Opening Statements

By Don C. Keenan

CONTRIBUTING AUTHORS

David Hoey, Ryan Skiver, Kevin Smith, Andrew Gould, Larry Kahn, & Mark Henness

ISBN-13: 978-0-9980073-1-1

Library of Congress Cataloging-in-Publication Data
Keenan, Don.
The Keenan Edge / Don Keenan
p. cm.
ISBN-10: 0-9980073-1-5

Printed by: Book Masters, Inc.
Printed and Bound in Ashland, Ohio

Balloon Press, 250 Park Avenue, 7th Floor
New York, NY 10177

DEDICATION

David Ball the country's leading forensic jury trial expert has been my friend for over 20 years. During that time we researched and confirmed the effectiveness of the Reptile as the most effective trial advocacy approach in the history of personal injury trial practice.

Many years ago David formulated the first template for opening statements. Since that time the opening template has undergone an evolution and will continue to evolve. This text includes the current evolution.

Because of David's early work and his dedication to the effectiveness of opening statements this book is dedicated to him.

Papa Don

ACKNOWLEDGMENTS

This book contains verbatim opening statements given in actual cases where I have been lead counsel together with some of the finest lawyers in the country who were referring attorneys in these cases.

The first opening statement is a bench trial where I delivered the opening statement. The remaining six opening statements in a variety of different cases were given by four of my referring attorneys. The Dean of the Keenan Ball College, David Hoey from Boston, Massachusetts, another was given by Kevin Smith from Charleston, South Carolina, another by Larry Calm of Seattle, Washington and Mark Hennes from Las Vegas, Nevada. The two remaining opening statements were given by my associate Andrew Gould based in Atlanta, Georgia.

I wish to acknowledge all of the above and as well the several hundred lawyers who have followed this format with actual opening statements in litigated cases.

Papa Don

ABOUT THE AUTHOR

Trial Lawyer

Don Keenan is the founder of the Reptile© who, with David Ball, co-created and co-authored the Reptile© book. During his 40 years of practice, Don has secured over 302 verdicts and settlements over $1,000,000, including ten over $10,000,000 and one over $100,000,000. Don has dedicated his practice to child and adult injury and wrongful death cases arising from medical negligence, products liability and premise liability, with the goal of making our society safer for children. He has handled cases in 47 states and three continents.

Child Advocate

Don strongly believes that a plaintiff attorney's duty does not end when justice has been secured for the child and family. Equally important is learning from the prevention lessons of the case and formulating a public awareness campaign to help prevent future injuries and deaths and, when necessary, push for legislation and regulations.

He calls this unique approach to law the One-Third Solution: One-third litigating the case, one-third public awareness on the prevention and one-third pushing for regulations and legislation. Examples of his One-Third Solution include his Playground Safety Project, which was featured on the Today Show for three years running, the Toy Safety Campaign profiled in USA Today and on Good Morning America; additionally the Imagine magazine summer 2005 issue featured Keenan and his One-Third Solution, as did Mercedes Momentum magazine in the winter of 2004.

Don has appeared on every major national news program including 60 Minutes, 20/20, Larry King Live, The Oprah Winfrey Show, Montel, The O'Reilly Factor, the Today Show, Good Morning America, CNN and National Public Radio (NPR) addressing children's issues.

Awards and Distinctions

- Selected by Oprah Winfrey as one of the "People Who Have Courage," notably for fighting for the rights of abused children for 30 years
- "Career Achievement Award for Public Policy and Child Advocacy" bestowed by Emory University
- Named by the National Law Journal as one of the top three medical malpractice lawyers in the U.S.
- Called "The Voice of the Voiceless" by The Atlanta Globe
- "Internationally renowned child advocacy lawyer" by Points North Magazine
- "A famous advocate for children" by Business Chronicle
- Ten-time recipient of "Top 100 Irish Americans" presented by Irish America Magazine
- 2007 Ellis Island Medal of Honor (only 100 awarded each year)
- 2008 Tradition of Excellence Award by the State Bar of Georgia
- Published the best-selling consumer book, 365 Ways to Keep Kids Safe, awarded a Gold Medal for "Best Parenting Book" in 2008 by Publishers Marketing Association

Professional Accomplishments

In 1992, Don became the youngest National President of the American Board of Trial Advocates. During his tenure, he led a delegation of lawyers to Czechoslovakia and later was invited to Russia to produce the first civil trial in the history of those two emerging democracies. In 1997, he became National President of the Inner Circle of Advocates, the most exclusive group of trial lawyers in the country. In 1999, he was given the prestigious Chief Justice Award for Civility and Professionalism, the highest award possible for a lawyer in Georgia. He now serves on the Advisory Committee for the National Judicial College in Reno, Nevada. In 1990 and again in 1992, he was named Trial Lawyer of the Year.

Significant Cases

Don successfully handled the U.S. Supreme Court case of Kathy Jo Taylor in the 1980's, which was the first case in U.S. history to establish due process rights for foster children. Again, in late 1999 he handled the nationally publicized case of Terrell Peterson, an abused foster child who was on the cover of Time magazine (Nov. 2000) and was the subject of the highest rated 60-Minute story of the year. Both cases resulted in significant changes in the rights of children in state custody. In 2006, he obtained the largest U.S. jury verdict for an abused child.

Trial Advocacy Books by Don C. Keenan

- Out-of-State Practice of Law; Pro Hac Vice, 1981, Harrison Publishing Company.
- Social Security Law; Procedure, 1986, Harrison Publishing Company.
- Obstetrical Medical Negligence, 1991, Law Press, Inc.
- Closing Arguments: Child Injury Wrongful Death, Volume I, 2004, Balloon Press.
- Closing Arguments: Child Injury, Wrongful Death, Volume II, 2008, Balloon Press.
- The Keenan Edge, 2012, Balloon Press
- The Keenan Edge 2, 2014, Balloon Press
- The Keenan Edge 3, 2016, Balloon Press
- The Reptile© in the Mist (and Beyond), 2013, Balloon Press

General Public Consumer Books

- 365 Ways to Keep Kids Safe, 2005, Balloon Press.
- First place, Benjamin Franklin Book Award by Publishers Marketing Association, Best Parenting Book of 2008.
- Outstanding Book by National Organization Exceptional Parent. Audio Tape Collection by Don C. Keenan
- Faces of the Future: How To Be A Better Lawyer For Children. 10 lectures re-mastered by TrialGuides.

Reptile Products by Don C. Keenan

- Reptile©: The 2009 Manual of the Plaintiff's Revolution, 2009, Balloon Press.
- Reptile©: The Keenan Law Firm Method to Witness Preparation (DVD), 2009, Balloon Press.
- Reptile©: Voir Dire - Keenan/ Ball Method of General and Case Specific Voir Dire (DVD), 2010, Balloon Press.
- Reptile©: The Ball Method of Opening Statements (DVD), 2011, Balloon Press.
- Reptile©: The 2009 Manual of the Plaintiff's Revolution (Audio Book), 2012, Balloon Press.
- Reptile©: The Ball Method of Opening Statements (DVD), New edition 2014, BalloonPress.

*To those courageous lawyers who were the first
to graduate from the Keenan Ball College:
You are the pioneers who blaze the path
for all who come after.
–Papa Don*

www.keenanballcollege.com

PREFACE

Everyone knows the Black Hats are anxiously awaiting every book and DVD we put out, so we have to be very careful not to spill the secret sauce in public.

From the Keenan Ball College (www.keenanballcollege.com) experience, we have learned the Opening Statement is one of the hardest pieces to learn and the hardest to execute. For years, lawyers have wanted "go bys" (that is, actual Opening Statements they could read through and assimilate to their own case(s)). While I wish to goodness I could narrate the thought processes that went into each of these Opening Statements – or at least go into greater detail about the format – I have infinite trust in each of you woodpeckers to read these seven examples and "get it."

While it is true that all of these cases fall into the category of "high end," after many years we've learned you can easily adopt a high-end anything to a low-end case. The rules are the same, the strategy is the same, the format is the same, and the outcome will be the same – no matter if it's a big case or a small case. That's been true since the very beginning.

A final note before you dive in is my involvement in these Opening Statements:

1.   I was lead counsel in all of these cases.
2.   With the exception of the first case (Goodin), I guided co-counsel in each case's Opening Statement.
3.   I was intimately involved in the many focus groups that molded the final Opening Statement, which was given to either the jury or the bench. Each Opening Statement was focus grouped at least 15 times.

I wish each of you continued success, and hope this book (which will become the sole textbook for the Keenan Ball College) will be of assistance to you.

Papa Don

TABLE OF CONTENTS

IMPORTANCE OF FOCUS GROUPS

Each of the opening statements contained in this book were focus grouped at least 20 times with each time getting valuable feedback from the focus group as to what changes needed to be made to make the opening statement perfect.

We continue through the many focus groups modifying and changing the content of the opening statement per the comments of the focus group.

To learn how to utilize focus groups for the purpose of creating a perfect opening statement please get a copy of the text "The Keenan Method of Focus Groups by Keenan Law Firm Associate Andrew Gould and Keenan Law Firm Director of Operations William Entrekin ." The book is a "how to" manual which includes how to select focus group jurors and a step-by-step process of how to conduct the focus groups.

The book can be obtained at www.reptilekeenanball.com.

The Keenan Ball College (KBC) has a two-day course on focus groups. Bait lawyers bring an actual case to the college and are instructed by experienced faculty members in hands-on application of the focus group process for their case. Each day at the college there will be an actual focus group so that the attendees can practice in front of an actual focus group.

Simply stated you cannot achieve a perfect opening statement without doing several focus groups.

DON KEENAN

GOODWIN CASE

Commercial Tractor Trailer Accident with injuries

DON KEENAN
Atlanta, GA

When Don Keenan talks about growing up in a town of 800 people in North Carolina (where his first generation Irish grandfather, Mayor for life, bravely and quickly desegregated the town's establishments when the "flames of segregation were blowing through the South"), he says – seemingly without any sense of double meaning – "There's no doubt I wanted to fight for the little people."

Those "little people" who became the focus of Keenan's work as a lawyer turned out to be children. For the last four decades he has dedicated his practice to child injury and wrongful death cases arising out of negligence, medical malpractice, products and premise liability. He's scored 322 case outcomes over $1 million, 12 over eight figures and one $100 million verdict. "There's never been a more successful national lawyer," he says proudly. He's handled cases in 47 states and three foreign countries. "In the last 25 years I've had more clients in many states other than in Georgia," he points out.

"There's no time in my life when I didn't want and I didn't know I'd be a lawyer," he relates. "My father died when I was just over a year old from a preventable boiler explosion, and my grandfather died from preventable malpractice by the town doctor."

He grew up with his mother and grandparents who were first generation Irish. Early on he learned about anti-Irish discrimination and believed he could help the underdog. However, in his first years at legal practice as a criminal defense lawyer, he "unfortunately never represented an innocent person." The experience was very discouraging and he decided to retire from law. "My life dream was shattered," he says, but serendipity called in the late 1970s. Atlanta was in turmoil over the murdered and missing children tragedy. Fifteen African-American mothers, frustrated because officials ignored them and the possible links between the murderers, stormed city hall. "I was approached by business leaders asking me to represent the mothers." These women wanted him to become their public spokesperson partly because he was white and could easily dispel racial tensions.

As their spokesperson, he was invited to appear on the Phil Donohue Show. He was introduced as "one of the country's leading child advocates." It took him a minute to realize Donahue was speaking about him. Then he walked into the role, which changed his life. He spoke so passionately about the forgotten children that immediately after the show his office phone lines lit up from parents "around the country wanting me to represent their injured or deceased children. I knew in an instant without any reflection that to represent children was the purpose in my life."

His first case was about a child in Kentucky who had worn flammable clothes and "almost burned to death." Keenan sued the clothes manufacturer. Then he was called by parents whose child lost an eye due to a defective toy. From there, his practice just took off. He remembers what his grandfather told him: "If one is passionate about what they do, success will follow."

Success has certainly followed Keenan.

In 1992 he became the youngest national President of the American Board of Trial Advocates (half the membership being civil defense lawyers and the other half Plaintiff's lawyers). During his tenure, he led a delegation of lawyers to then-Czechoslovakia and was later invited to Russia to demonstrate the first civil jury trial in the history of those two emerging democracies. As the youngest member ever inducted into the Inner Circle of Advocates, he became its national President in 1997. This is an exclusive group of Plaintiff trial lawyers numbering only 100 in the United States. In 1999, he was given the prestigious Chief Justice Award for civility and professionalism and in 2008, received the highest award from the Georgia Bar Trial Section, the Tradition of Excellence Award. He's been named by the National Law Journal as one of the top three medical malpractice lawyers in the country.

But these are not the criteria he points to as his success.

In 2009 he became bored as he connected with "some people who were attuned to the role of the subconscious in our decision-making opinions. This is something that was never recognized in trial practice but acknowledged and used in driving public relations, marketing, politics and even theology, everything except the profession that has to persuade 12 strangers."

Keenan linked up with a national jury expert and "we tried to prove it wrong. We traveled around the country and, in five years, did 22 twoday focus groups in nine separate states. We were trying to prove that juries will decide cases logically and fact-based. We found that not to be true. They don't check their emotions or life experiences on the doorstep of the courthouse." Keenan ended up writing a book about this and began to conduct seminars which have been attended by more than 7,000 lawyers nationwide.

"In 2013 I decided it wasn't enough to lecture lawyers. I had to mentor them," he says. He created the Keenan Ball Trial College. The class size is restricted to eight lawyers who bring their cases and, with trained lawyer faculty, separate the work into all aspects of the case such as damages and voir dire. He has now graduated more than 120 lawyers from the college with a course being taught somewhere in America every two weeks.

Keenan now works with a network of 7,000 lawyers around the country, while 6,300 read his weekly trial blog. "When I go to work on a case, I get together with our lawyers and we have adopted a new trial technique. It's not really a new way but the origin of Tort law, which says that the purpose is to compensate a person – but the second purpose is to deter a Defendant from doing it again. It's always been the law, but Plaintiffs haven't used it." Keenan does, and is now directing the writing of a text entitled Essentials of Tort Law. Lawyers in this network have told him that they have now documented recoveries of over $7 billion in settlements and verdicts using his technique.

All of the cases impact children in one way or the other. He explains about his recent case in Boston resulting in a $6.6 million verdict for a woman who was traumatized by a rape but that her children were also traumatized as well. "The long-lasting impact is on our kids," he says. "Ninety percent of our cases our lawyers handle are essentially children cases."

Keenan explains how he approaches juries. "When jurors are composed in a wrongful death case they think about their parents dying. It's not to manipulate them but to touch the true core of us as people. The lawyers must tell them they are the conscience of the community." Keenan advises referral attorneys in his network to put themselves into the situation to better understand their clients' cases. For example, he went to truck driving school to learn about it because many of his cases involve trucks. "I also attended a garbage truck training school because I had such a case. Juries want to see us as human and caring," he explains. "Many of my peers don't share my idea of teaching my referring lawyers, because they might not refer additional cases. But that's not been my experience; they want and need the collaboration," he says.

Besides he got to the point that he couldn't handle all of the cases as lead counsel, so that he was setting up a new form or referral called a "consult," which means doing focus groups for the cases, prepping for depositions, the mediation and template for trial – everything except providing his actual presence. "On the consult cases I don't have to go anywhere," he exclaims from his Florida beach house where he often works, although he has offices in Atlanta and Los Angeles as well.

Within a three month period, two of Keenan's consult cases resulted in two 15 million dollar verdicts then the following month a $9 million settlement. No more than one third of his practice consists of this new form of "consulting" referring attorneys. "That's because I want to try cases," he says. "But when I get something that works, I spread it through my many referring attorneys through workshops and my blog." He uses a Keenan Law Firm Office Management Template. "If you want to work with us this is how you do it, this is how to get greater verdicts and settlements by training these attorneys. Long after I'm gone this consult concept will finally be accepted," he says.

Keenan has been called Johnny Appleseed on steroids with the way he spreads his concepts of better lawyering.

He's also been nicknamed "Papa Don" which is endearing to him because that's what he called his grandfather, Papa. "I challenge anybody on who gets more Father's Day cards than me. Each year I say I'm not going to cry this year and every year I cry." He receives the cards not only from the children whose cases he worked. In 1993, he started the Keenan's Kids Foundation, through which five employees and hundreds of volunteers raise and distribute close to $1 million in cash and inkind donations. The Foundation also published an award-winning book, 365 Ways to Keep Kids Safe – the title coming from Oprah Winfrey who gave Keenan the prestigious "People with Courage" Award in 2009. The Foundation also built the Murphy House, a home for 23 children with Down's syndrome and other disabilities. The Foundation has created safety projects and conducted public advocacy campaigns and collects items and clothes for children at risk. "We were the second largest giver of children's clothing in the aftermath of Katrina," he says. Another project that gained the Foundation much attention is the bologna and cheese sandwiches which they make and give to shelters, although Keenan says for health reason it's now turkey and cheese sandwiches.

The Foundation has won numerous national awards and he is a seven-time recipient of "Top 100 Irish Americans" presented by the Irish American Magazine. But the most treasured award outside law that he's received was one of the only 100 Ellis Island Medals of Honor presented in 2007. To be the recipient, a person must have ethnic parents who enabled him or her to get the success they dreamed of for their offspring. "This is an award for my great grandparents and mother," he says. "Never would I have been able to do what I've done without standing on their shoulders."

STATE OF SOUTH CAROLINA   COURT OR COM-
MON PLEAS
COUNTY OF CHARLESTON   2009-CP-10-05861

CURTIS GOODWIN, Plaintiff

V.

CLEVELAND DEVON HEYWARD and CHRIS THOMPSON SERVICES LLC, Defendant

TRANSCRIPT OF RECORD

JULY 28, 2011
Charleston, South Carolina

BEFORE:
THE HONORABLE DEADRA L. JEFFERSON, JUDGE

APPEARANCES:

MR. DON KEENAN, ESQUIRE
REPRESENTING THE PLAINTIFF

Anne Bouley Meyer, RPR
Circuit Court Reporter

(Opening Statement.)

THE COURT: Ready to proceed?

MR. KEENAN: May it please the Court.

THE COURT: We can dispense with opening arguments unless you think those are absolutely necessary because I have already reviewed the file.

MR. KEENAN: Your Honor, they will be very short, but I hope that they would be helpful to Your Honor.

THE COURT: You may proceed.

MR. KEENAN: Your Honor.

Every year, more than 60 citizens of the Charleston community, while safely driving their vehicles, are blindsided by tractor trailer trucks driving recklessly and unsafely. This is according to the South Carolina Department of Highway safety.

What brings us here today are the safety rules that protect all of us when we are on the highway with large tractor-trailer trucks beside and behind us. We will have a number of witnesses, but I want to direct the court to the three essential rules.

First, these safety rules will apply to any tractor-trailer company anywhere in the United States.

Safety Rule No. 1: Their equipment must be safe in order to protect everyone on the highway from mayhem and death.

Safety Rule No. 2: The tractor-trailer company is responsible, under the laws of this state and the federal government, to hire qualified drivers, train them properly and then to supervise them in order to protect everyone on the highway from mayhem and death.

Safety Rule No. 3: The final rule is that once those drivers are trained, they must follow the safety rules of operating their vehicle, their large rigs, on the highway to protect everyone on the highway from mayhem and death.

Let me tell you the story of what happened in this case – if you remember one thing, Mr. Goodwin is a community martyr, he took a bullet for the community

And very briefly, Your Honor, the evidence that brings us here today, under safety rule No. 1, the equipment, is that this truck had not been inspected for three consecutive years. It did not have proper state certificate to operate on the highway to begin with.

And last but not least, Your Honor, two of the tires on this truck were flat. And every single one of the tires did not meet code. In other words, they're almost bare.

So clearly Safety Rule No. 1 was violated. Safety Rule No. 2, that is the drivers must be qualified, supervised, and trained, was also violated. This particular company, Your Honor, the evidence will show, had no background checks, had no training protocol, and had absolutely no supervision protocol that put this 22-year-old boy on the highway in this large tractor-trailer truck with this company not knowing that in his short life he had been involved in two fairly large wrecks, and he has seven violations of moving vehicle laws, one of which was speeding at 153 miles an hour.

So clearly any responsible tractor-trailer company having looked at this fellow would not have hired him to begin with, let alone put him behind this rig unsupervised and untrained, dictates the very outcome that we have.

Now Rule No. 3 applies, of course, to the driver following of the safety rules. And, Your Honor, if I can just point to the diagram that will be accredited by the experts; this particular catastrophe occurred five days before Christmas in the year 2007 on a Friday afternoon on a busy highway.

And the safety rule for any of us, let alone a tractor-trailer company, is that when you pass on the right, as you'll see in that diagram, Vehicle Number Two, when you pass on the right, you must know that the lane that you are going into is absolutely clear.

Not only was it not clear, but the Defendant driver, traveling in excess of the speed limit, going 75 miles an hour, smashed into the cab of Mr. Goodwin, thereby causing him to lose control and flip on his vehicle's side and crash into and ruin the guardrail itself.

Imagine if Mr. Goodwin was not driving his box truck and it was some teenager in a car? If you remember one thing: Mr. Goodwin is a community martyr, he took a bullet for the community.

Now it's un-contradicted that he did not have the right-of-way. In fact, the fellow, the Defendant, pled guilty to improper lane change. But, Your Honor, the other thing that perhaps is a little more difficult to dig out of the record, which we think is significant is a danger that lurks behind all of this bad conduct: The mountain of lies that are told here.

First of all, the driver said, well, the reason why this happened – and he reported it to the original investigator who called up on his behalf – he said, well, I had my cell phone and I got distracted. Then, he comes to the deposition and swears under oath, well, I may or may not have said that to the investigator, but it's not true because I had my cell phone in the cradle the whole time.

The second, and more glaring, is the fact that he didn't say a word other than, I cut the guy off, I'm sorry, at the scene. Said the very same thing to the interviewer, gave justification of being on the phone. Yet when he came to his deposition several years later he said, oh no, that's not right at all. Those drivers out there were cutting me off. It wasn't my fault at all.

But, Your Honor, the most disturbing, and the last fact on the liability, is what he said on deposition – which of course is sworn testimony in the record (page 50) – when he said that his employer, Mr. Thompson, instructed him to do certain things.

This is what he says at Line 8: "Mr. Thompson, he was trying to get me to change everything that I had said. It was a lie, what he was basically telling me to say. I don't remember specifically what he said, but he said to lie. He wanted me to say something that wasn't truthful."

So, Your Honor, we have a systematic breakdown here of of not only the safety rules that protect all of us on the highway, but also the safety rules that protect justice being done.

Now just a word or two, Your Honor, on the damages. We should point out that on this given day, five days before Christmas, while it is Mr. Goodwin that occupied the position of a dump-truck on that diagram that got cut off, it could have been a school bus, it could have been a car full of women going to an event, it could have been a motorcycle rider.

In fact, Your Honor, if you look at the dynamics, if it was anyone other than a dump-truck driver, they would have certainly been killed. This is a random victim. This company needlessly endangered the public. And it just so happens that Mr. Goodwin is the one who was seriously injured for the rest of his life.

The simple truth, Your Honor, is that Mr. Goodwin is a community martyr; he took a bullet for the community.

I hope that this brief, factual Opening Statement has been helpful to Your Honor.

Your Honor, if I may, we've prepared a summary that's very short, it's in a little bit better organized fashion, in fact we filed this. With the Court's permission, may I bring it up?

THE COURT: I have one I believe.

MR. KEENAN: Not this, Your Honor.

THE COURT: What is that?

MR. KEENAN: It's actually our evidence brief we are to use throughout our testimony.

THE COURT: I think you gave me one.

MR. KEENAN: That's the exhibits, I believe.

THE COURT: Yes, sir.

MR. KEENAN: Thank you, Your Honor.

THE COURT: You're welcome.

MR. KEENAN: Your Honor, I have already discussed the first three pages there. And I now want to just touch on this – believe me in a manner of just a minute or so – page 3, beginning with Roman Numeral II, the damages: You'll hear from Mr. Goodwin, born and raised in South Carolina, he has four children from one woman. I think sequentially, Judge, it's important to know that of course this catastrophe occurred in December of '07 and the love of his life and mother of his children passed away in April of 2009.

So since that time, he has two grown children away from the home, but he has been the sole parent for the 10- and 11-year-old who, Your Honor, you will hear from very briefly.

According to the South Carolina tables, Mr. Goodwin has at least 40 years to go until his expected date of death. Your Honor, you'll see there are four categories of special damages set forth; loss of income past, loss of income future, past medical costs, and future medical costs, all of which, Your Honor, will be testified to.

And I just need to make one or two comments about the highlights; the medical treatments to date, the major things that have occurred to him, primarily a very, very serious operation to his shoulder he still has not recovered from.

And then after a year or two of non-responsive medical treatment for his neck problem, they finally had to do not a 1, not a 2, but a 3-level fusion. You'll hear from the neurosurgery, Your Honor, dotting the i's and crossing the t's, that, in fact, this collision was the approximate cause of that damage solely and completely.

The life-care plan – of course the medical bills total nearly $200,000. The life-care plan of almost $200,000 is, Your Honor, primarily the epidural blocks and steroid blocks that he has got to have continuously in order to be able to have any semblance of quality of life.

The loss of income is very definite, $144,218, which will be substantiated through the economist. He did have a benevolent employer, that while he could never drive a truck again, he was given light duty. That light duty then disappeared, and he has been unemployed, and you'll hear a number of witnesses, Your Honor, that will substantiate that this fellow with 40 years of life to go is not employable in any category at all.

Finally, Your Honor – because of what I said in the beginning, I have not done this in some time, but because South Carolina law has a very clear basis for punitive damages, based on these clearly intentional choices to violate the safety laws – we would request your Honor's consideration for a punitive damage verdict at the end of this case to clearly send a message that lying and reckless conduct is not to be permitted on the highways of this state.

Thank you, Your Honor. Our witnesses to follow, some of which will be five minutes, some will be a little bit longer, but we are going to hit the highlights and give this case to Your Honor very quickly.

Thank you, Your Honor.

THE COURT: Yes, sir.

***

DAVID HOEY

WAHLSTROM CASE

Parking Lot Rape

DAVID J. HOEY
North Reading, MA

Nationally recognized in civil trial practice, David J. Hoey has passionately advocated for elderly victims of abuse and neglect for the past two decades. Having first joined the revolution in 2010 and by 2012 teaching it to others, Hoey has quickly become a staple in the fight against tort reform. As the Dean of the Keenan Ball College (www.keenanballcollege.com), Hoey strives to help students master winning techniques not only inside the courtroom, but in their practices as well.

Hoey is the President of the Law Office of David J. Hoey, PC, where he practices in the areas of nursing home abuse and neglect, assisted living facilities and injuries to the elderly. He has recently been voted as a member of the Board of Directors to the National Citizen's Coalition for Nursing Home Reform (NCCNHR), based out of Washington, D.C. NCCNHR is the nation's largest advocacy organization for nursing home residents. NCCNHR is celebrating its 37th anniversary this year "Working Together for Quality Long Term Care."

Hoey is author of "Prosecuting Nursing Home Cases in Massachusetts" (Lawyers Weekly), "Most Common Mistakes Attorneys Make in Prosecuting Nursing Home Cases" (ATLA), and he is currently working with West Publishing on a nursing home litigation manual. Hoey previously has spoken on nursing home bankruptcy issues and Medicare Medicaid issues in nursing homes. He was also a speaker for the New England Patient Rights Group on "Nursing Home Awareness;" MCLE's Personal Injury Year in Review (Nursing Home Section); and National Business Institute's seminar on Nursing Home Malpractice in Massachusetts. He is a past chair of ATLA's Nursing Home Litigation Group. He was elected by his peers as A Rising Star/ Super Lawyer in 2005.

The Law Office of David J. Hoey, PC (HOEYLAW) attempts, through litigation, to improve quality of care and quality of life in Massachusetts nursing homes and assisted living facilities. Hoey is also admitted in the State of New Hampshire.

(Opening Statement.)

<u>Good morning, everyone</u>.

I. INTRODUCTION

Every four minutes and 45 seconds, someone is a victim of a violent crime inside a commercial parking lot or garage. This is according to the U.S. Department of Justice's Statistics for Crime, years 2004-2008.

What brings us to this Suffolk County courthouse today are the safety rules that protect us from violent crimes anytime we go to a commercial parking lot or garage.

These safety rules, like all safety rules, will protect us only if they are enforced. It is up to you, the jury, to determine what is reasonable – as the Court will tell you later. We will submit three simple safety rules to help determine what is reasonable. <u>You may want to write this down:</u>

Safety Rule No. 1: Commercial parking garage owners and managers must take **all reasonable steps** to prevent crime on their premises…to protect all of us.

Safety Rule No. 2: Commercial parking garage owners and managers, after a violent crime has occurred, must install **cameras to <u>deter</u> a repeat crime in the same area**…to protect all of us.

Safety Rule No. 3: Commercial parking garage owners and managers, after a violent crime has occurred, **must concentrate the security force in the area of the crime**… to protect all of us.

II. STORY OF WHAT THE DEFENDANT DID

Now let me tell you the story of what happened in this case:

A multi-level parking garage was connected to the Radisson Hotel Boston [<u>show picture</u>]. It was not exclusive to the hotel guests. It was located in Boston, used by hotel guests and visitors, restaurant goers, students, theater attendees, and workers in the surrounding area.

<u>This is important to know</u>: Many crimes, including violent crimes, occurred at the hotel and parking garage complex over the years, **with spikes in 2006 and again in 2008**. Many of the crimes on the property occurred after midnight.

In 2008, 43 out of 54 reported crimes occurred in the parking garage. That's 80 percent of crime on this property. At some time prior to June 2008, the security staff on the night shift consisted of **four people, one of whom was designated to the parking garage itself**.

However, security staff was cut down from four to one, no longer designated to the garage. Crime at this location was foreseeable; it could be armed robbery, aggravated assault, theft or rape.

The parking garage has six parking levels with 700 spaces.

There is one video camera in the hotel lobby that looks into the parking garage elevator vestibule. There are **no other cameras on any other parking level**.

The security for the hotel and garage during the overnight shift was one guard, who did one walk-through of the entire complex, which takes him 45 to 90 minutes.

On April 19, 2009, a hotel employee coming to work sees a guy walking around the first floor of the parking garage. She is concerned; she calls the front desk to send security right away.

Security comes to the second floor and does not see this guy.

Ten to 20 minutes later, **another** hotel employee is on her way into work and is approached by this guy. He assaults and rapes her next to her car.

The one lobby video camera records the guy coming and going from the elevators before and after the rape. Security later extracts still images of him from the videos.

The following day, the security director emailed out an alert (through a security network he was a member of) using the pictures from the videos. He also provided pictures of the rapist to his security guards, so they could keep an eye out for this rapist.

Three days after the rape, the Boston police detective in charge of the investigation of this rape saw the alert and contacted the security director, upset with him for not checking with her first, and informed him that before he disseminates any information to check with her first.

After the April 19 rape of their own employee, the hotel added another security guard for the overnight shift and installed two new video cameras in the garage elevator entrance only.

Twelve days later (more precisely, 11 days and 21 hours), on May 1, there were two security guards on duty for the overnight shift. At 2 a.m., both guards locked themselves in the hotel lobby, as per security policy. No one is assigned to watch the security cameras, including those two recently installed cameras on the first floor.

A lighting technician at a nearby night club goes to retrieve her car after work in the hotel parking garage. The rapist, who 12 days earlier, raped the hotel employee, enters the parking elevator lobby and gets on the elevator. A few moments later, the night club employee gets on the same elevator.

As she begins to exit the elevator, she is suddenly and without warning grabbed by this guy, who pulls her and shoves her into a stairwell. For the next seven to eight minutes, he rapes her, then steals her money and flees.

Police are contacted and she is sent to the hospital.

Days after the May 1 rape, the hotel hires a public relations firm to deal with the media. The PR firm tells the media (<u>you may want to write this down, too</u>): "**At the time of the second rape, Boston Police Department had in fact asked hotel officials not to publicize the first rape to guests or employees.**"

This, ladies and gentlemen, is **<u>untrue</u>**. BPD never said the hotel couldn't inform their guests or employees; **in fact**, the hotel did notify their employees but chose not to notify the hotel guests or other garage users.

The guy you've just heard about is Jose Rivera III. At the time, he was 280 pounds, 6 feet and 1 inches tall, and he is serving 15 years in maximum security prison. He pled guilty to five counts of aggravated rape, two counts of assault and battery, assault with intent to rob and unarmed robbery for both rapes.

The Plaintiff in this case, the May 1 victim, is Kira Wahlstrom.

If you remember one thing from this part of the story: If the Defendant did what they were supposed to do – such as increasing lighting, installing cameras, increasing the number of guards and walking patrols – back in 2006 or 2008 when the spikes in crimes occurred, neither the April rape or May rape of 2009 would have occurred.

The simple truth is, when a rape occurs, a second rape on the same premises with the same rapist, is preventable.

III. WHO WE ARE SUING AND WHY

Let me tell you who we are suing and why.

Kira Wahlstrom, the May 1 rape victim, is suing the owner of the property, JPA IV Management Company, Inc., a Massachusetts for-profit corporation who is the trustee of a business trust that has owned this property for years.

She's suing JPA I Management Company, Inc., another Massachusetts for-profit corporation, which JPA IV hired to manage the day-to-day operations of the hotel and parking garage. They managed this property since 2003.

JPA I Management Company, Inc., later hires LAZ Parking Limited, LLC, to help with the operation of the parking garage. LAZ was established in 1984, it is the largest parking lot and garage company in the U.S., with more than 1,300 locations in 23 states. At the time, Laz operated 200 locations in Massachusetts, 50 of them in Boston.

She's suing them for violating the safety rules that protect all of us when we use commercial parking lots and garages.

She's suing all three, because all three share a duty to protect Kira Wahlstrom and others by following the safety rules:

Garage owners and managers must take all reasonable steps to prevent crime on their premises…to protect all of us.

Garage owners and managers, after a violent crime has occurred, must install cameras to deter a repeat crime in the same area…to protect all of us.

Garage owners and managers, after a violent crime has occurred, must concentrate the security force in the area of the crime…to protect all of us.

But the Plaintiff is not the only one that alleges that the Defendants were negligent.

The Defendants in this case are suing each other, alleging that each of the other was negligent, thereabout causing Kira's rape.

IV. UNDERMINE DEFENSES

Before we brought this case to you here at trial, we had to determine **five very important matters:**

First, we had to take into consideration whether the additional measures after the April 19 rape were reasonable.

After the April 19 rape, in order to keep their customers safe, all they had to do was:

Provide warning and notification of the risk and educate everyone about the crimes or rapes, not just their employees.

They must put cameras on each floor to deter crime.

They must employ enough staff at peak crime hours.

They must have staff that are supervised and trained/not abandon the garage.

However, keeping in mind that if the Defendants had done what they were supposed to do in 2006 or 2008 when the spikes in crime occurred – instead of decreasing their security staff – neither the April nor the May of 2009 rapes would have occurred.

Ladies and gentleman, it is not necessary to determine what steps or measures would have prevented the rapes. It is simply your job to determine if what was done was **unreasonable**…

Because what they did **didn't work**. What they did simply **wasn't enough**. They had the capability, the money, and should have had the knowledge to do more, but they chose not to. <u>The system failed.</u>

The second thing we had to determine before we came to trial was whether the BPD's instructions after the April 19 rape to the Radisson Hotel Boston's security did, in any way, tie the security department's hands and stop them from implementing more reasonable security.

So we spoke to the BPD detective in charge, who gave "the instructions" about her conversations with security personnel. Although she admitted being upset and having raised her voice, she did so because the April 19th victim's name was given out in violation of the rape shield laws. We further learned that there is no evidence that BPD ever told anyone from JPA or LAZ that they could not warn, notify, or educate their customers, or otherwise secure their premises and protect their customers or employees.

Additionally, this BPD detective also provided safety tips for the hotel, to help protect their patrons and staff.

Perhaps the JPA security director got spooked by the police and perceived that his hands were tied, so they took no other steps to protect their customers. Or perhaps the PR firm they retained after the May 1 rape came up with a different story.

Next, we had to consider whether Rivera could have been stopped; whether added security guards or increased lighting or cameras on each floor or any combination thereof would have made a difference.

So we decided to ask the guy who did it. We met with him – but that's all I'm allowed to tell you about that right now. We wanted to have him testify before you, but he is incarcerated for 15 years and it is safer if he stays where he is.

We had to figure out LAZ Parking's role and duty to protect the customers and employees... Whether they could legally be an ostrich and put their head in the sand, or whether they had a duty or obligation to help with the security and safety of patrons using the garage.

It is up to you, the jury, to determine if LAZ had a duty and breached it.

Their contract with JPA said that – <u>and you may want to write this down as well</u> – they were hired to "**assist and consult with the operations**" of the garage. They helped with security in the past, as well.

And lastly, certain issues had to be resolved by the court.

For example, you will hear the name "Radisson" a lot. JPA was a franchisee of Radisson, which gave JPA the right to use the Radisson name. The Court has ruled **as a matter of Massachusetts law** that Radisson Hotels International, Inc., is **not** responsible in any regard.

JPA still maintained complete control of the operations and staffing of the hotel and garage. Likewise, with regard to the City of Boston and its Police Department, the Court has ruled they have governmental immunity.

The simple truth is, when a rape occurs, a second rape on the same premises by the same rapist is preventable.

V. CAUSATION AND DAMAGES

Now, let's turn our attention to the most important reasons we are here, which is to assess the damages, the harms and the losses of Kira Wahlstrom. Now, that part of the case will be handled by my co-counsel, Don Keenan. Let me give you a preview of what that evidence will be.

Make no mistake about it; the damages that I speak of are permanent and deep, they will last every minute of her life. It has been six years and for six years the Defendants have denied she was raped. For six years, they denied responsibility and do not want to accept accountability. They blame someone and something else, including each other.

I suspect that the Defense will point out that she sought no treatment for seven months, and that's correct, and that tells all of us how deep and suffocating the damages were because she was in a stupor. You know most rape victims never come forward, ever. She did, she fought through all the obstacles, tried to do it herself, and when she realized she couldn't, she turned to counseling.

And the sad fact is, she went through repeated failures and treatment that didn't work before finally – after nearly five years – she found a therapist who had the key. Since that time, the therapy has been unrelenting. And this therapist will tell you all the things that were tried until finally, we are on the right road. But it is a long road. It's a road that will last the rest of her life, because there is no cure for abuse or rape victims – there is only coping, must of it through self-help exercises.

We will hear from a nationally known clinical specialist in psychiatric nursing and a professor at Boston College with more than 40 years of experience. She helped develop the very first certification for S.A.N.E., which stands for "Sexual Assault Nurse Examiner," which can now be found in almost every hospital in the country.

She will help us understand that Kira will always have to live with the fears, the smells, the images of that night, and she will just cope with this rape and its effect upon her from now on. There are triggers that bring it back; someone coming up behind her, the color green, a door slamming behind her. Although it was only approximately seven to eight minutes, those minutes in Kira's life feel much longer and haunt her every day of her life. These facts and their effect upon her life will be substantiated through Kira's friends, therapists and family.

We will learn of the stages of PT grief:

Denial

Advocate/disassociation (denial/anger?) – tried to be an advocate early on to get the message out; the media will be here to be an advocate for her, that's how important these issues are.

Anger – becomes compounded

Cure myself (denial/anger?)

Counseling (bargaining?)

Medications (depression? – lack of sleep – anxiety)

Per Kübler-Ross model (Denial Anger Bargaining Depression Acceptance)

Ladies and gentlemen, please listen carefully to the damages she suffered through her words, and emotions, and that of her treating counselors.

This is a lifetime. It ranks among the most egregious harm that a human can go through. Part of her needs is for them to accept responsibility, so it's up to you to show them how. Thank you.

**

<u>RYAN SKIVER</u>

FARMER CASE

Armored Truck Crash Injuries

RYAN SKIVER
Scottsdale, AZ

Ryan Skiver graduated from Ohio University in 2001 with a Bachelor of Business Administration and a major in Finance. He attended Southwestern Law School and graduated in the top 20 percent of his class and participated in Honors Trial Advocacy Program. Ryan is the Assistant Dean of the Trial course for the Keenan Ball College, including being an instructor who has taught at all 3 locations: Atlanta, Austin, and Las Vegas.

Ryan was born and raised in Ohio with three sisters and a brother. After graduating college, Ryan moved to California for law school. After law school, Ryan moved to Arizona to practice.

Ryan enjoys traveling, playing sports, outdoor activities and adventure sports, as well as spending time with his family and his two Labrador Retrievers.

(Opening Statement.)

I. STATISTIC

Every hour a person is injured by a large truck in this country, according to the Federal Motor Carrier Safety Administration.

II.   OPENING SNIPPET

What brings us to the Maricopa County Superior Courthouse today are the safety rules that protect all of us from large commercial vehicles when they are maneuvering through an intersection. And these safety rules, like all safety rules, will protect us if jurors choose to enforce them.

III.   SAFETY RULES

Safety Rule No. 1: Trucking companies must follow their own policies and procedures to prevent injury and death to us all.

Safety Rule No. 2: Trucking companies must supervise their drivers to prevent injury and death to us all.

Safety Rule No. 3: Truck drivers must stop for red lights to prevent injury and death to us all.

IV.   STORY

Now I'm going to tell you the story of what happened in this case:

Since their start in Canada in 1995, Garda armored truck company spreads to become a multinational company on multiple continents.

In 2005, Garda armored truck company expands into the United States.

Garda armored trucks learns U.S. regulations require a Commercial Driver's License (CDL) for drivers of a Commercial Motor Vehicle that weighs 26,001 pounds or more.

Garda orders its armored trucks to weigh 26,000 pounds – one pound less than the federal requirement for hiring drivers with a CDL.

Three years later, in August of 2008, Garda Armored Trucks hires Aleem Shaheed Howard.

Six months later, on February 12, 2009, Garda armored trucks does a performance review of Aleem Shaheed Howard.

Garda Armored Truck's performance review of Aleem Shaheed Howard notes "at times, Aleem appears to be tired and at times non-attentive."

Garda Armored Trucks puts this performance review in Aleem Shaheed Howard's file, and does nothing further.

Garda Armored Trucks chooses to put Aleem Shaheed Howard back behind the wheel of their armored trucks.

Less than three weeks later, Aleem Shaheed Howard drives a Garda armored truck southbound on 59th Ave., in the middle lane of traffic.

As Aleem Shaheed Howard approaches Peoria Ave., the traffic light turns yellow.

The traffic light is yellow for four seconds. (Pause for four seconds with four fingers in the air slowly counting down.)

Aleem Shaheed Howard keeps his foot on the accelerator, as the work truck to his left slows down and stops before the intersection.

Garda's armored truck driver keeps his foot on the accelerator.

Garda's armored truck driver sees a grey SUV in the intersection, facing towards his truck, begin to turn left.

Garda's armored truck is five feet from the intersection when the light turns red.

Garda's armored truck crosses over the crosswalk.

The grey SUV does a U-turn, and avoids the armored truck.

Garda's armored truck driver swerves to the right.

Garda's armored truck goes up on its driver's side two wheels.

Garda's 26,000-pound armored truck careens towards a green minivan stopped for the light facing east.

Garda's armored truck slams (clap) into the driver's side of the green minivan stopped for the light.

Garda's armored truck, which weighs more than five times as much as the 4,800 pound green minivan, spins the green minivan 180 degrees.

Garda's armored truck continues on and crashes (clap?) into a white convertible, impacting three more vehicles – for a total of five vehicles.

But the woman in the green minivan was injured the worst.

Garda's armored truck, which is wrapped in armor designed to ricochet machine gun bullets, finally comes to a stop.

There is significant damage to both the armored truck and to the green minivan.

We can be thankful that nobody was killed in this crash.

We represent the driver of the green minivan, Stephanie Farmer, and her family; her husband Keith Farmer and their daughter Breanna Farmer.

Luckily there was a video camera pointed towards the intersection.

Ladies and gentlemen, I am going to show you the video of what happened that day, just as I have described it to you.

See where I am pointing with my laser pointer? Here is the Garda armored truck.

Now, this is important, watch closely because he going to go through this video rather quickly.

Do any of you need to see that again?

The video happens in real time, but we also have an enhanced version that slows it down for you to slow-motion with better color/contrast, if you would like to see that as well?

Now I'm going to show you a still picture that was taken from this video.

First lighthouse phrase with bumper sticker:

The simple truth is, human life is more valuable than Garda's bottom line.

V.   WHO WE ARE SUING AND WHY

Now let me explain who we are suing and why.

We are suing the Garda West, CL Corporation doing business as Garda Cash Logistics, and one of its drivers, Aleem Shaheed Howard.

Now let me explain how this happened.

We found seven key reasons (clean reasons):

Reason #1: Garda Armored Trucks' policies and procedures or safety rules require them to do a driving record check in every state where an applicant has had a license for the past three years. Garda Armored Trucks knew that Aleem Shaheed Howard had a driver's license in Arizona and California and drove oil trucks in Texas, but chose not to do a driving record check in all three states.

Reason #2: Garda Armored Trucks' policies and procedures or safety rules also require them to get records for the prior two years of drug and alcohol testing for applicants, but Garda Armored Trucks chose not to get all of those drug and alcohol testing records for Howard. **(Schnurstein Depo at 241:16-245:23)**

Reason #3: Garda Armored Trucks' policies and procedures or safety rules also require them to only hire employees with a good employment history, and Garda Armored Trucks admitted that Aleem Shaheed Howard's employment history for a 24-year-old who had worked 13 jobs in three different states did not constitute a good employment record. **(Schnurstein Dep. At 165:19-166:25)**

Reason #4: Federal regulations require Garda Armored Trucks to track drivers' work hours to make sure that they are not exceeding the limit. Garda Armored Trucks admits that they knew Aleem Shaheed Howard had a second job, but Garda Armored Trucks chose not to track Aleem Shaheed Howard's total hours of work between his two jobs. As you will hear from a National Trucking Expert, this is to prevent fatigued or tired drivers. Garda Armored Trucks' own performance review shows they knew Aleem Shaheed Howard appeared to be tired and non-attentive. **(Schnurstein Depo at 183:5-186:8)**

Reason #5: Garda Armored Trucks chose to give its armored truck drivers a route to run each day. You will hear that Aleem Shaheed Howard knew that he would be done with work for Garda Armored Trucks as soon as he finished that route.

Reason #6: Garda's armored truck ran the red light, which we knew when we had an expert slow down the video from the intersection and discovered that Garda's armored truck was still five feet behind the stop line for the intersection when the light turned red, as you can see in this photo.

Now I'm sure the Defendants will get up here and give the excuse that the grey SUV in the intersection on the yellow light should have yielded to their armored truck running the red light.

So we considered that excuse, which brings us to:

Reason #7: Garda Armored Trucks performed their own internal investigation, they watched the video you just saw, and you will be convinced just as Garda Armored Trucks was by the evidence that this was not an accident but a major preventable crash.

So there you have it, CASE OVER.

YOU DECIDE.

Now you decide if our community deserves better than having to constantly watch out for the mayhem of armored trucks running red lights.

And you decide the right way and wrong way to act in our intersections, because we all know that conduct rewarded is conduct repeated.

Second lighthouse phrase with bumper sticker:

If you remember one thing, human life is more valuable than Garda's bottom line.

VI.   CAUSATION AND DAMAGES

Now let's turn our attention to the most important reason we are here. And that is to assess the damages to the Farmers'. That part of the case will be handled by my co-counsel, Mr. Keenan.

Let me give you a preview of what that evidence will be…

Make no mistake about it, the damages that we speak of are permanent, deep, and will last every minute of Stephanie, Keith, and Breanna's lives.

As you have heard, since the date of the crash on March 6, 2009, it has already been more than six years and 10 months.

And for that entire time, the Defendants have denied they are responsible for the crash, even though Garda Armored Trucks' own internal documents say the opposite.

After watching the video you saw earlier, the police officer investigating this crash determined how the crash happened and informed Garda Armored Trucks.

And then Garda Armored Trucks own Branch Manager sent an email to management saying, "*bad news from the Glendale police department…the video from the cameras show the light turned red before we entered the intersection.*"

You decide what that tells us about the largest armored truck company in the world.

Now, let's look at what has happened to Stephanie over this nearly seven year period of time.

Let's start with the top of her head. We will learn from the experts in this case that when Garda's armored truck smashed into Stephanie's minivan, she hit her head on the driver's side beam, and suffered a head injury.

We will also learn that Stephanie suffered a jaw injury that caused pain in her teeth and her jaw. We will also learn that Stephanie now has a TMJ injury, which the doctors will describe to us. We will also learn about the problems Stephanie now has with her teeth not lining up for chewing. We will hear about the brace she has to wear in her mouth when she sleeps and the jaw pain every day with every meal.

Next let's move down to Stephanie's neck. We will hear that Stephanie went through multiple different types of conservative care, but after they all failed she was forced to undergo surgery on her spine in her neck. The surgeons had to remove a disc from in between two of her vertebrae.

We will learn that Stephanie's neck surgery had a complication, and she had to go through another surgery for a dura repair. We will hear how Stephanie has had to go to an anesthesiologist for pain management to quiet the pain from the nerves in her neck. We will learn how Stephanie has to have needles stuck into her neck with electrical charges to burn the nerves coming out of her spine to try to dull the pain for six months to a year at a time.

We will learn how Stephanie's knee suffered a traumatic injury from the crash that has required seven surgeries over the past seven years, with each surgery becoming more invasive. We will learn that the partial knee replacement performed last year did not work, and how Stephanie just recently went back in for surgery to have a total knee replacement. We will learn how the doctor had to cut open Stephanie's knee with a scalpel, saw off a piece of her thigh bone and shin bones to implant a metal joint connecting her leg back together. We will learn about the year-long recovery from this surgery and the uncertainty about how it will turn out and when Stephanie may need another one.

We will hear about what Stephanie's life will likely be like when she is 80 or 90 years old.

We will also learn the most devastating damage to this family. Stephanie and Keith's daughter Breanna is severely developmentally disabled. Bree is deaf and she has the mental capacity of a 3-year-old. Bree eats through a tube and requires 24/7 care, and all the physical demands that come with the responsibility of caring for this precious child.

We will learn that Stephanie and Keith have always taken care of Bree for the past 20 years in their home, refusing to give up on her. And we will learn that Stephanie and Keith continued to take care of Bree for four years after this crash, in the hopes that Stephanie might be able to recover to the point where Stephanie could again provide 24/7 care for Bree.

And lastly, we will learn that Stephanie could no longer meet the physical demands of caring for Bree, and so Stephanie and Keith then had to make the devastating decision to put their daughter in a group home.

We will hear how this damage has been the worst thing to happen to the Farmers as a result of this crash.

I can't believe I actually have to say this, but we also expect that the Defense will make the **repugnant, disgusting argument** that Stephanie and Keith took this devastation to their family as an opportunity to put Bree in a group home because they wanted to be rid of the burden of taking care of her.

We will share with you that after those 20 years, four of which were after this crash, Stephanie and Keith were forced to make the heart-wrenching decision to do what was best for Bree to get the care she needs 24/7, because of Stephanie's injuries she could no longer provide.

We will get to learn how Bree's life will look going forward, as she has been ripped from the only home she has ever known with her family for her whole life, to be placed with strangers in an unfamiliar home. We will hear how nobody can explain to her why her mother is not there to hold her in the middle of the night and rub her ears while she tries to fall back asleep.

You will decide whether to hold Garda accountable for choosing to violate their own policies and procedures or safety rules.

Then you will decide the value of those damages to Stephanie, Keith and Breanna. You will decide how important these safety rules are to our community. Your verdict will speak to how our community values families and our right to be safe when we are on our streets.

Third lighthouse phrase with bumper sticker:

The simple truth is human life is more valuable than Garda's bottom line.

Let's get to work. Thank you.

***

KEVIN SMITH

B.E.C CASE

electric power line contact, wrongful death, and brain injury

KEVIN SMITH
Charleston, SC

Kevin Smith grew up in Charleston, South Carolina, where he attended The Citadel on a full athletic scholarship. Kevin is an instructor at Keenan Ball College and has taught at all 3 locations: Atlanta, Austin, and Las Vegas.

From there, Smith went to law school in Boston, Massachusetts. Upon returning to Charleston, he began a practice of helping injured victims that would define his adult life.

Smith is a delegate for Charleston on the board of the South Carolina Association for Justice. Aside from the practice of law, he serves as the chairman of the board for the Trident Literacy Association, a local nonprofit that teaches adults to read and write.

(Opening Statement.)

PRIMARY RULES

May it please the Court. Roughly every 72 hours, an American worker is killed by a power line. This is according to the National Bureau of Labor and Statistics.

What brings us together in the Berkeley County Courthouse are the safety rules that protect each and every one of us against the danger of electrocution. These safety rules will protect us ONLY if our courts choose to enforce them. The safety rules we will be discussing protect all of us as we are working and carrying on our daily lives around power lines. They surround our homes, farms, business, highways, schools, even our courthouses… Power lines are found nearly everywhere people are.

There are three safety rules that apply in this case.

Safety Rule No. 1: The NESC: A power company must construct and maintain its power lines at least 18.5 feet high above farms or lands with animals to prevent injury to people or death by electrocution.

Safety Rule #2: The Code of Federal Regulations: A power company must inspect their power lines to ensure that they are at Code height to prevent injury to people or death by electrocution.

Safety Rule #3: A power company must tell the truth about its compliance with electrical safety laws when reporting to the federal government to prevent injury to people or death by electrocution.

STORY OF WHAT THE DEFENDANTS DID

This is a story 20 years in the making.

We need to go back to 1993. McClellanville. A power company installs a new high voltage power line. The location…a horse farm. There are about 100 horses on the farm. They raise horses, they teach people to ride and jump, and they also raise crops. The power company puts up a power line near one of the old wooden barns, in an area where horses are ridden. No one notes what the land is being used for. No one notes how high it is required to be. No one tells the workers how high it is required to be. Even after it's put up, no one measures the power line to make sure it's at the right height. This is their standard procedure. The evidence will show they are doing what they always do.

Ten years passes and no one has ever inspected the power line to make sure it's at code height. The power company sends it workers out to the farm twice that year; still, no inspections for height compliance. The lineman who is supposedly inspecting these power lines doesn't even know how high it's required to be. The lineman also doesn't know they are required to be looking to see if the use of the land has changed, because that might affect the required height.

It's now 2005, 12 years after the power line was put up. The power line still has still never been inspected to make sure it's at code height. The CEO for the power company and other high-level executives sit down to complete a safety form for the government. The CEO sees the section called "compliance with safety codes." He doesn't know how many power lines his workers are inspecting, and he doesn't know what they're required to look for. He does know that even if the inspections are taking place, they are not patrolling all of their overhead power lines annually. He signs off and certifies that all overhead power lines are being patrolled annually. The power company gets federal tax dollars if they say they are in compliance.

The power company sends its employees out to this power line on the farm six more times. No one measures the power line to see if it's at the required height. No one has ever made sure the power line is at the height required by law. The lineman assigned to the farm's district concedes he did not inspect the power line for code height…he still doesn't know how high they are required to be.

In the fall of 2007, plans are underway to host a charity event out at the farm. A staging company is hired to set up tents, chairs and a dance floor. Promotional plans are made.

It's now 2008, 15 years after the power line was erected. It's time again to fill out the government safety forms. The CEO still doesn't know how many power lines have been inspected…but he knows that if they are inspected, no one is noting whether the power line is up to code. The people he represents are inspecting these power lines have still never been told how high they are required to be. They still don't know they are supposed to be looking to see if the use of the land has changed. He signs the form, this time certifying that inspections are taking place AND that the linemen are looking to see if the use of the land has changed. Federal funds are at stake each time he completes these forms.

Just four months after the last government safety forms were signed, the charity event is about to happen on the farm. It's now called Thornhill Farms, Healing Ministries. They still do farming, they still have livestock, and they still have horses. On this day, four men are setting up a tent. Three of them are day laborers. The men get the tent put up. It has four poles around the edges. It has another pole in the center. That pole has a tip at the top, called a spire. The spire fits through a little hole in the canvas and holds the tent up high. Once the tent is erected, the spire cannot be seen by anyone standing beneath the canvas.

Now that the tent has been put together, the men are instructed to move the tent. Each of them picks up one of the supporting poles. They don't lift the tent up high. Just enough to move it. They walk the tent to the new spot. They are told to move it again. This time in the direction of the power line – but from where they're standing, they can't see it. The people directing them are standing on the ground and from their point of view, it looks like there's plenty of room. The men pick up the tent. Just as they start to shuffle it backwards, the tent spire hits the high voltage line.

Everyone around hears a loud pop. The high-voltage electricity surges through their bodies. Two of the men are killed. The current goes through the other two, leaving entrance and exit burns. All four men fall to the ground.

The power company finally measures the power line and it's more than a foot and a half too low.

The evidence will show that had the power line been at the height required by the NESC, the tent these men were moving never would have touched the energized line. If the power company had just done the inspections they said they were doing, they could have caught it, and I submit to your Honor that this never would have happened.

WHO WE ARE SUING AND WHY

We are suing Berkeley Electric for four reasons.

The first reason we are suing Berkeley Electric is because Berkeley Electric violated the safety rule requiring the power line to be at least 18.5 feet high.

We know this because the measurements taken the day the men were killed show the power line was far below code.

The law sets minimum heights for power lines. It does this based off what the land is being used for. If the land is used as a farm, this is the required height: 18.5 feet high. If the land is used for riding horses, this is the required height: 18.5 feet high. Or, if the land and has vehicles over eight feet high, this is the required height: 18.5 feet.

We spoke to the woman who owed the property when the power line was first put up. She not only grew crops but she also raised horses. She even had a riding course set up to teach people to do the riding and jumping competitions. They rode horses in the area around the power line. She had vehicles over eight feet high and those vehicles were driven in the area of the power line.

We also spoke to an engineer named John Dagenhart. Mr. Dagenhart worked on the committee for the National Electric Safety Code. For those working with electricity, this book is the Bible for safety issues. This is where the height requirements come from. He pointed us to the chart that sets the required heights. We have the chart for you to look at. It's easy to read and understand. You'll see the power line was required to be at least 18.5 feet at all times.

Please keep in mind, the 18.5 feet requirement applies to the very lowest point of the power line. In this case, the point of contact was not at the lowest point. If the lowest point is 18.5 feet high, then the other parts – including where this tent hit – are going to be higher. You'll see there would have been plenty of room for the tent if the lowest point was at least 18.5 feet high.

The evidence will show that had the power line been at the required height, the tent these men were moving would not have hit the energized line, and this never would have happened.

The second reason we are suing Berkeley Electric is because Berkeley Electric violated the safety rule requiring them to inspect their power lines for Code height.

This means…they missed every opportunity to ensure the power line complied with the NESC.

Berkeley Electric concedes they are required to inspect their power lines for height. This requirement comes from the NESC, the Code of Federal Regulations, and BEC's own safety manual. Berkeley Electric has told us this power was never measured after it was put up. And, it wasn't measured over the next 15 years. The Code of Federal Regulations specifically requires that inspections of power lines must include a determination of whether the line complies with the height requirements of the NESC. Berkeley Electric told us this power line has *never* been inspected for compliance with the National Electric Safety Code. They also told us this isn't the only one. That's in part because they don't tell their linemen what the code requires and it's not written down anywhere.

The evidence will show that had Berkeley Electric inspected this power line, they could have raised it before the men were killed and others were injured.

The third reason we are suing Berkeley Electric is because Berkeley Electric repeatedly lied to the government, which we submit to your Honor prevented

others from knowing the unsafe conditions in time to step in to rectify the violations and save lives.

We have copies of the forms Berkeley Electric completed. We know who all signed off them. We know that the scores Berkeley Electric gave themselves warrant that they are inspecting all of their overhead power lines for Code height each year. The scores they gave themselves over and over mean, and I quote, "all overhead power lines patrolled annually." Berkley Electric concedes that they have never patrolled all of their overhead power lines annually.

And since they don't tell their linemen how the high power lines are supposed to be, even if they do inspect the power line, they wouldn't know what they are looking for. And these government safety forms, well, I only mentioned two of them. You should also know they actually do these every three years. We have copies of these safety forms dating all the way back to 1990. You will hear Berkeley Electric has been giving themselves these perfect marks over and over again.

The final reason we are suing Berkeley Electric is because Berkeley Electric refuses to accept responsibility for what they did. So we're forced to bring them to trial.

UNDERMINE NEGLIGENT DEFENSES

Now, before we came to trial, the parties did extensive discovery and dove deep into the issues.

One of those issues concerns the event organizers. They are the ones who told the men where to move the tent. We needed to know if Berkeley Electric was still responsible, even though the event organizers directed the men towards the power line.

The law says, first of all, that **power companies** must use "the highest degree of care" in <u>constructing</u>, <u>maintaining</u> and <u>inspecting</u> their power lines. That's the legal standard in this case; the highest degree of care.

The law also requires power companies to think about how to keep people safe, to think about what's foreseeable. So we took the sworn testimony of several employees of Berkeley Electric. We asked them about foreseeable harms. We asked them specifically, is it foreseeable that people would work around energized power lines without having them shut off? They said yes, it is foreseeable that people would work around their power lines without having them shut off. This includes not only the laborers working with tents in this case, but also people using machinery to drive posts into the ground, or using a boom truck to pour concrete. Those are pretty obvious examples...

You'll hear from our expert that also within the foreseeable class is anyone who is helping a neighbor put up a flag pole, or hang a sign, or trim their trees. If this is going to happen, and Berkeley Electric knows this is going to happen, then our expert will explain the one and only thing that Berkeley Electric has do is make sure their high voltage power lines are at least as high as the law requires. The evidence will show that's why Berkeley Electric is required to inspect their power lines, so they can make sure they are in compliance with the law and reduce the chances of death by electrocution.

With this in mind, we wanted to know if Berkeley Electric could blame the event planners for doing what Berkeley Electric admits was foreseeable. The law says when someone does something wrong, but someone else comes along and makes a mistake later, the first person is still responsible if what the other did was foreseeable. In other words, if Berkeley Electric violated the safety rules by having a low hanging power line and a faulty inspection plan, and they know people will work around their power lines without having them turned off, that does not excuse their violation. The evidence will show that Berkeley Electric has one job to do: Make sure their power lines are high enough and in compliance with the law.

If someone is killed, I submit to your Honor that our laws hold that Berkeley Electric can't excuse themselves by saying, well, so what, he shouldn't have been around it in the first place. Our expert will explain that would negate the whole purpose behind the height requirements of the NESC. To quote the law, it says, "Power companies and their employees, **even more than all other people**, ought to know the great danger of electricity. They ought to take care to see that their wires, which convey electric current, are properly guarded, so as to prevent injuries to persons and property. This duty is incumbent upon them under the law of this state."

You're going to hear the Defense talk a lot about OSHA and those regulations. You're going hear about the things the OSHA investigator says Mr. Fortney's employer, a company called Stage Presence, did wrong. You'll hear that there is something called the 10 foot rule... that people should not go within 10 feet of an energized power line. OSHA cited Stage Presence for failing to teach them to not encroach on the 10 foot territory. The OSHA investigator has testified that had he found that either Mr. Fortney or Robinson knowingly did anything wrong, he would have issued separate citations to Stage Presence for employee misconduct. And that wasn't done here. Our expert on visual matters will explain that neither Mr. Fortney nor Mr. Robinson had any concept of the danger. She'll also explain that from where the party planners were standing, it would have looked like the tent had plenty of room. And remember, the law on foreseeability says this is not a valid defense because they were simply doing what Berkeley Electric already knew was foreseeable.

You're going to hear Berkeley Electric say they aren't liable because they didn't cause the line to be this low. Our expert, Mr. Dagenhart, will explain to your Honor that they did cause the line to be this low. He will testify that one of the reasons the line was too low is because the Berkeley Electric crew used too much line, and this caused it to sag over 12 feet from the connection points on the poles. Now, Berkeley Electric will claim something must have hit the line and caused it to sag. You'll see from the evidence that couldn't be true. You'll hear that nothing is going to stretch a power line that much. And, we have evidence that the damage to the line they will point to was actually caused 5 years before the men at Thornhill Farms were electrocuted. The evidence will show this comes as a surprise to Berkeley Electric…because they weren't inspecting the lines and weren't even looking for these types of things.

Berkeley Electric is also expected to take the position that they had no actual knowledge that the line was too low. We agree with that assertion. The reason is that the evidence will show that Berkeley Electric's lawyer contends the line was only required to be 14.5 feet at the lowest point. Now again, our expert will show your Honor the chart and he will explain why 18.5 feet is what the law requires. So we agree they didn't know it was too low…and that's because number one, they had the required height wrong and number two, they didn't EVER inspect the line for compliance with the NESC.

Berkeley Electric has told us their inspection program consists of basically two parts. First, they say they tell their linemen to inspect the power lines they are working around. In other words, if they have to service a power line, they say their lineman also inspect that power line. And second, that they hire a company to do pole inspections. And remember, the Code of Federal Regulations requires these inspections to include a determination as to whether the power line complies with the height requirements of the NESC. We already discussed how the linemen aren't told how high the lines in their district are supposed to be. And even if the linemen call the home office to ask, Berkeley Electric doesn't write down anywhere what the law requires for height of their power lines. And regarding the pole inspections, the evidence will also show they are just that, pole inspections. We have a copy of the contract with the pole inspectors and nowhere does it say anything about inspecting power lines for height. Although there's a vague request to "report unsafe conditions," the pole inspectors aren't asked to determine of the heights comply with the law… and just like the linemen, the pole inspectors aren't told how high they're required to be.

Finally, Berkeley Electric contends in their Pre-trial Brief that maybe the NESC didn't apply that day. That it applied every other day since 1993, just not this one. They explain that there is some question as to whether or not the area around the power line was a construction zone…because they were "constructing" tents. Mr. Dagenhart will explain to your Honor that first, there is no mention of a construction zone free-for-all in the NESC. However, the handbook describes some leeway under two limited scenarios. First, when people are wiring a house or a building and doing tests on the lines before they are insulated and permanently installed, the requirements are relaxed just so the tests can be done. Of course, if the tests come back okay, the final installations must be up to code. The second scenario discussed is when construction companies bring out big cranes to erect buildings, they don't have to go and raise the power lines hundreds of feet in the air above these huge cranes. That's it. Berkeley Electric will contend the laws didn't apply simply because men were putting up tents that day. Our expert will testify that this is when the laws matter the most – when you're putting up tents on a farm for a charity event, that's precisely the time the height requirements in the NESC matter the most.

You've probably figured out by now that the parties see this case differently. On the one hand, we will be discussing what we submit will be clear violations of nearly every statutory and industry safety rule that applies to this case. The Defense on the other hand will treat this trial as a character assassination. Their paid expert, Eric Jackson, has worked on this case for six years. Yet he still refuses to tell us how high this power line was required to be. He told us this is because he doesn't know what the land was being used for at the time the high voltage power line was built – despite having read the deposition of the land owner who describes in detail what the land was being used for.

You don't have to go to law school to know how dangerous high voltage electricity is. One touch and it can kill any one of us. We submit to your Honor, did Berkeley Electric exercise the highest degree of care and act in accordance with the danger? If they didn't, the families deserve a verdict. If not, then these legal doctrines...these safety rules…they don't mean a thing, and Berkeley Electric gets a free pass.

DAMAGES

At the end of this trial, we will ask your Honor to decide how much money should be in the verdict. You'll hear how the electricity entered John Robinson's chest and exited through his foot. He fell to the ground and was taken by helicopter to the emergency room. He spent three days there, over concerns with his heart. He required follow-up care for his wounds, and counseling to help deal with the memories of his dead friends. Still to this day, Mr. Robinson is reminded of all this by the burns on his chest and foot.

John Fortney was electrocuted by high voltage electricity; 14,400 volts of electricity surged through his body and caused his heart to stop beating. This is seven times the electrical current used to put people to death in this state. He endured attempts to save his life at the scene, in the ambulance and at the emergency room. John was pronounced dead about an hour later.

John left behind two beautiful children. One piece of advice he gave them was, "Don't turn out like your dumb old dad." His little girls, Gina and Emma, miss their dumb old dad and they want his life and his death to have meant something. Emma was asked, "When you lost your dad, what did you lose?" She responded, "I lost my best friend." We will ask your Honor to place a value on that; a value that reflects the emotional pain and sorrow that will last with both of his children for life.

B   erkeley Electric is going to tell you what a horrible man John was. Their lawyer is going to tell you his kids haven't lost anything. And, if cross examination goes anything like the depositions, you'll actually see Defense counsel try to convince these girls that their dad never even loved them. But, if you remember one thing about John Fortney, it's that the evidence will show John had just gotten a steady job, he was trying to make amends, trying to be a better man, a better father…until he was killed. Clearly he had not arrived, but for him, he had come so far…and now Gina and Emma are without a father, they'll never have the chance to have a relationship with him. Their children will never have a chance to even know him.

As I said before, there is a stark contrast in our cases. The Defense is far more interested in running down the people they kill, insulting their families, and minimizing the value of human life. The evidence will show you Berkeley Electric is totally ignoring their gross violations of the NESC, which are designed to prevent the very thing that happened here. I submit to you, it's nothing but arrogance.

Full and fair compensation will have the effect that the people in our tri-county area are not a magnet for this kind of thing.

We ask that your Honor doesn't deny us a verdict that's fair, reasonable and substantial.

　　***

<u>ANDREW GOULD</u>

THOMAS CASE

wrongful death medical malpractice

ANDREW GOULD
Atlanta, GA

Andrew Gould grew up in the mountains of North Georgia in a small town called Chatsworth. After graduating from Murray County High School, he attended the University of the South in Sewanee, Tenn., where he was a four-year starter as the kicker for the football team, proctor of his dormitory for two years, member of Delta Tau Delta and member of the Order of The Gownsmen. Andrew is an instructor at Keenan Ball College and has taught at all 3 locations: Atlanta, Austin, and Las Vegas.

From there, Gould attended law school at New England Law: Boston. During his tenure there, he co-founded the Education Law Society and clerked for Boston Legal Services: Elder Law Department. During his summers, he clerked for two Plaintiff firms in the North Georgia area.

Gould joined the Keenan Law Firm in Sept. 2012. Since coming aboard, he has participated in several trials and taken many depositions. Also, on several occasions, Gould has had the opportunity to speak on topics such as depositions, rules, demonstrative evidence and focus groups throughout the U.S.

(Opening Statement.)

PART I

More than 400,000 patients die every year in the United States due to preventable medical errors inside hospitals; this is according to a study published in the *Journal of Patient Safety*, which relied on medical records and studies published from 2008 to 2011.

What brings us to the Jefferson County Courthouse today is the standard of care, which you will hear is comprised of a series of patient safety rules, which protect all of us when we or our loved ones receive care at a hospital. These patient safety rules, like all safety rules, protect us if juries choose to enforce them.

Safety Rule No. 1: A hospital must make sure that its nurses are properly trained, to prevent harm or death to patients.

Safety Rule No. 2: A supervising physician must make sure that residents-in-training are properly trained and supervised to prevent harm or death to patients.

Safety Rule No. 3: A resident physician must be trained to contact his or her supervising physician when he or she recognizes a new medical complication that he or she is unfamiliar with to prevent harm or death to patients.

PART II

Now let's walk through a timeline that will help us understand what happened in this case. The events on this timeline, and the corresponding medical records, begin on August 15, 2008. The events take place at University of Louisville Hospital. (timeline). The patient who died was named Glenda Thomas. We represent the Estate of Mrs. Thomas, and that is her husband Dennis Thomas sitting right over there.

If you remember one thing, **people who have this neck surgery don't die from suffocation.**

PART III

Before coming to trial, we did an extensive investigation to determine how this happened; based on what we learned in that investigation let me tell you who we are suing and why.

We are first suing the University of Louisville Hospital for violating the patient safety rule, which requires hospitals to have properly trained nurses caring for patients in post-operative care. We know they violated this patient safety rule because their own nurse, Nurse Glenn, admitted she was not trained that a hematoma, which is simply blood accumulating under the skin like a bruise, and swelling of tissues in the neck, could cause suffocation and death (first video). The University Hospital's own nurse expert will tell you this is basic, well-known knowledge that she expects all nurses are expected to have (second video clip). Nurse Glenn did not have this well-known knowledge.

We then learned how it was Nurse Glenn obtained this basic knowledge. She told us that a year or so after the death of Mrs. Thomas, she decided to research on the internet, at her home, how something like this could happen. She will tell you the hospital did not instruct her to do this or suggest that she do this (third video clip). That is the first reason we concluded that the hospital did not have properly trained nurses.

We also know the hospital did not have properly trained nurses, because none of the three nurses who cared for Mrs. Thomas ever utilized the chain of command (CoC) when they should have recognized their patient was not receiving the necessary care that would have saved her life. A CoC applies to work situations that have life or death consequences, such as police officers, firemen, the military and hospitals. And it is well known within each of those entities, what the specific CoC is. The CoC required any of these three nurses to go as high up the ladder as was necessary to provide safe care to the patient if any of them believed a resident either lacked the knowledge to safely care for the patient, or was simply ignoring her concerns and not providing the necessary, safe care to the patient. None of them ever did.

You will hear Nurse Stepp explain why she wanted a surgeon to see Glenda after the drain had fallen out. She will tell you that because of Glenda's medical history (specifically an airway complication during a prior surgery), she was concerned about the potential for an airway complication after the JP drain fell out. But after her repeated attempts to reach Dr. Kazmi, who did not get a surgeon to see Glenda before the transfer, Nurse Stepp never utilized the chain of command to make sure a surgeon saw Mrs. Thomas before she was transferred out of the PACU.

That is when we learned, as you will hear from the hospital's corporate representative during this trial, the Univ. Hospital had no written policy for the chain of command (fourth video clip). A CoC that is not in writing and is not specific is not a CoC, because it is subject to multiple interpretations, as you will see in this case. That is the second reason we concluded this hospital did not have properly trained nurses.

We are also suing the NIKY Group (a private medical practice run by a group of neurosurgeons) and its supervising/real doctors in charge of the Univ. Hospital's Neurosurgery Residency Program for violating the second patient safety rule, which requires them to properly supervise and train its resident-in-training neurosurgeons who cared for patients inside the teaching hospital at the time Mrs. Thomas died.

We know they did not properly train their doctors, since neither the fifth- or sixth-year doctor in training ever treated this life-threatening complication as an emergency until it was too late to save Mrs. Thomas' life. We know this because even after the sixth-year doctor in training reviewed the second x-ray, he went home rather than ordering emergency surgery or calling his supervising/real doctor for help (fifth video clip) – even at 9:30 when Mrs. Thomas' condition got worse, the fifth-year doctor in training did not put an emergency order on the transfer to the OR because she still did not recognize the seriousness of the situation.

We also know the Defendants did not properly train these doctors in training because neither doctor in training treated this as a life-threatening situation – despite the individual risks they knew Mrs. Thomas had before doing this surgery, especially as it related to airway compromise. One risk factor, foreshadowing the hours to come, was an airway difficulty/complication she suffered following a prior surgery. It was right there in the clinic's pre-surgery records when they were determining how to approach her surgery. (Show 4 exhibit) It was also in the pre-surgery anesthesia record. (Show 5 exhibit)

Nurse Stepp had both these records inside the PACU, and her testimony is she believed the prior complication was due to a (luh-RING-go-spaz-um), which you will hear is a breathing difficulty or complication that can occur during or after surgery. She testified that this is why she wanted a surgeon to look at her, and why she did not want her to go to the general floor, especially after the JP drain had fallen out. Then you will hear from Glenda's husband Dennis, who will tell you that both him and Glenda had made this prior complication a big point with her doctors prior to the surgery.

Both doctors in trainings had access to the same records Nurse Stepp had before the surgery started. In spite of this, neither recognized the life-threatening potential, even after the JP drain had fallen out. Neither contacted a supervising/real doctor to discuss the possibility of an airway complication given this known history. That is how we determined no one properly trained these doctors in training.

We also know the NIKY Group did not properly supervise these doctors in training because after reviewing the fifth-year doctor in training's personnel file, we learned there were numerous emails and reports from her past, and from the Louisville Univ. Hospital itself, informing them of her misrepresentations about her whereabouts while she was supposed to be on-call, and her misrepresentations in the medical records about the care she was providing to her patients. (show 1 & 2 exhibits) In one email from 2007, the chief of the residency program at Louisville Hospital was made aware how the fifth-year doctor in training had been flaunting at a recent social event how she was "untouchable" and could "get away with anything." (show 3 exhibit-email). Yet she was the only neurosurgeon left in charge of caring for Mrs. Thomas the night Mrs. Thomas quit breathing. Everyone else had left the hospital.

The fact she was left alone further shows the lack of supervision because, as you will hear from the witness stand, she was the only surgeon caring for Glenda not capable of performing surgery by herself. Meaning, she could not perform any emergency surgery without direct supervision, yet she was alone the night of the code. (sixth video clip) The closest surgeon capable of performing the emergency surgery was 15 minutes away. That is how we concluded NIKY did not properly supervise these doctors in training.

We are also suing the NIKY Group for violating the third patient safety rule, which requires them to create an environment inside this teaching hospital where doctors-in-training are comfortable contacting their supervising neurosurgeons when he or she recognizes a new medical complication that he or she is unfamiliar with, or has never treated before.

You will hear from the witness stand how this safety rule is even more important inside this teaching hospital, because regardless of their year – third-, fourth-, or fifth-year resident – all resident doctors are "doctors in training," not independent, real doctors. That is why there are attending/real doctors, which we learned are simply the supervising doctor to the doctors in training. Or, as the Defendant's own neurosurgeon expert will tell you, are the life lines whenever the doctors in training encounter something new, or note significant changes with the patient.

We know they violated this patient safety rule because neither of the doctors in training ever called their supervising/real doctor before the code at 9:40, and no supervising/ real doctor recalls receiving a phone call from either of them about Mrs. Thomas. The 6th year doctor in training will tell you he does not recall calling a supervising/real doctor (7th clip). Given this, we asked the 5th year doctor in training, and she will tell you she never called anyone either (8th clip). And finally, the on-call supervising/real surgeon will tell you he does not recall anyone calling him prior to the code (9th clip). That is how we concluded neither of the doctors in training ever contacted their supervising doctor about Mrs. Thomas prior to the code at 9:40 pm. Simply put, no real surgeon ever saw Mrs. Thomas after her surgery.

The last fact you will have to consider as it relates to why we are suing the Univ. Hospital and NIKY Group, is that on the night of the code, one of the real doctors told Dennis and Glenda's brother Keith, flat out, before any lawyers were involved, "This is malpractice." You will first here the doctor deny ever saying this, but then you'll get to hear from Dennis who was there during the conversation.

For all these reasons, we sued these Defendants.

PART IV

However, before coming to trial, there were still a number of questions we needed to answer.

First, when examining this case in its totality, we had to look at the fact that an anesthesiologist saw Mrs. Thomas before being released to the general floor and determine whether he should be held responsible for releasing her. We first learned that the JP drain is strictly a neurosurgeon issue. We then learned from Defendants own witnesses that a surgeon must sign off before a patient is released from the PACU. You will hear that an anesthesiologist can see a patient, but a patient cannot leave the PACU until the surgeon signs off on the release. Then our anesthesiologist expert will explain that it is the responsibility of the neurosurgeon to monitor Mrs. Thomas closer once she was moved to the general floor, especially when he or she knows the JP drain had fallen out.

In fact, the treating anesthesiologist who saw Mrs. Thomas, when asked, told us that had he been notified about any of Mrs. Thomas's corresponding respiratory difficulties after she was moved to the general floor, he would have brought her back to the recovery room for closer observation, and notified the surgical team immediately. But he was never notified. Based on all that, we determined he was not responsible.

We then learned that this type of neck surgery is one of, if not the, most common type of neck surgery performed by neurosurgeons. We also learned that this 6th year doctor in training had performed this type of neck surgery many times before on many patients before Mrs. Thomas.

Once we knew that, we looked at the Defendants' excuse that this complication was so rare that it could not be expected or prevented. So we asked our experts, who agreed that this complication is rare. However, our experts & Defendants' own neurosurgeon expert told us that even though it was rare, any real neurosurgeon would know about it since it is a well-known, life-threatening complication. That is how we learned that while rare, had these doctors in training and nurses contacted a supervising, real doctor, he would have known to look for and rule out this well-known, life threatening complication.

This excuse of theirs led us to ask how often a patient dies from suffocation following a neck surgery such as the one Mrs. Thomas had. So we asked two of the Defendants' own experts, and both told us that they had never heard of or read about a patient dying from suffocation following this type of neck surgery.

Remarkably, you will hear from the witness stand Defendants' own neurosurgeon expert tell you that he can recall 2 patients from his past that had suffered the same complication following a similar neck surgery. And in both those instances, both patients were taken to the O.R, both patients were properly and safely intubated and both patients survived.

That is because, the simple truth is, people who have this neck surgery don't die from suffocation.

We then needed to know, how did Mrs. Thomas die from suffocation following this neck surgery? If the Defendants' excuse that this hematoma grew in a split second is true, then her death could not be prevented and the Defendants would not be responsible.

That's when we learned that the JP drain is used to drain excess fluids and blood away from an incision site. We learned that the JP drain, at the time it fell out of Mrs. Thomas's neck, was in fact draining excess fluids and blood away from her neck incision site.

Then our pathologist expert explained to us that this hematoma with Mrs. Thomas did not grow in an instant, as the Defendants' suggest, but rather, grew gradually over time. He told us that as the hematoma grew, it slowly constricted the airway, causing the breathing difficulties we saw in the timeline, until it ultimately cut off her breathing to the point where no oxygen got to the brain and she suffered the severe brain injury and died.

That is when our anesthesiologist expert explained to us, that because the JP drain had fallen out, it is important to have a plan to reevaluate the patient on the general floor to make sure a hematoma did not compromise the airway. He will also explain to you how imperative it is to take a patient to the O.R. and intubate the patient when you see the signs of this airway complication, such as the second x-ray at 8:22 p.m. which clearly showed the swelling & possible hematoma in the neck, or the worsening condition at 9:30. Because, as you will hear, if you wait around, and the airway becomes too constricted, it makes intubating the patient, and sustaining the breathing, impossible. You will see our expert use this animation to explain this in greater detail. (play animation) Given all this information, we concluded that this hematoma grew over time, not in an instant.

Now, we also expect the Defense will show you how Jessica, Mrs. Thomas's daughter, went home around 8:15-8:30 p.m. We expect they will argue that because she left when she did, things could not have been as serious as the Thomas's are now alleging, because if they had been, Jessica would not have gone home.

You will hear from Jessica, and she will explain how from 6 p.m. until she left around 8:15-8:30 p.m., she was repeatedly questioning the nurses and the fifth-year doctor in training about (among other things) the swelling in her mother's neck, her mother's complaints of pain, and her mother's difficulties breathing. And each time she expressed a concern about what she was witnessing, she was told it was normal and reassured that her mother would be okay and that they were taking good care of her.

Jessica will explain how she began to believe that her constant stress and anxiety around her mother was causing more harm than good for her mother. Given that, plus the fact that her father would stay with her mother overnight, she decided to trust the medical team and went home, believing that everything she had witnessed was normal for this common neck surgery, and that her mother would be okay.

PARTS V - VII

This brings us to the most important reason we are here. And that is to assess the damages to the Thomas family. While Mr. Keenan will handle that part of the case, allow me to give you a preview of what that evidence will be.

As you can see from the timeline, it has already been nearly seven years and 10 months since Mrs. Thomas died on Aug. 21, 2008. And for that entire seven years and 10 months, the Defendants have outright denied they have any responsibility for her death. Going so far as to attempt to guilt Mrs. Thomas's own daughter for trusting the Defendants' own medical team when they repeatedly assured her everything would be okay.

(BE SOFT) In order to do your job, and evaluate the life of Mrs. Thomas, you will need to know who Glenda was. So you will first hear from our economist who will explain to you, had Glenda survived, what her reasonable annual income would have been over the remaining years of her life expectancy of 82 years, which would have been 32 years since she was 50 at the time of her death.

You will then hear from members of Glenda's family and Glenda's friends who will share stories with you to help you better understand who Glenda was to so many different people, not to garner sympathy, but to assist you in your job.

You will then hear from her husband Dennis, and her daughter Jessica who will walk you through her final hours at the hospital. You will hear from them about her repeated complaints of pain in her chest, and struggles to breathe. They will walk you through, as only they can, the vivid moments that led up to her code. How Dennis raced out of the room screaming for help when his wife of 33 years was no longer breathing. You will hear from them their reaction when they were told that their wife and mother was so brain damaged, she would never recover.

You will be asked to evaluate all this evidence, and provide a verdict for that loss. For that grief. For not only the life of Glenda Thomas before the cervical surgery, and the life she would have lived had she not died, but the long hours we saw on the timeline that ultimately led to her severe brain injury and death.

You will also be asked to render a punitive verdict against these Defendants for what the evidence will show was a reckless disregard for the life and safety of Mrs. Thomas.

Simply put, you will be asked to hold these Defendants responsible, because, if you remember one thing, people who have this neck surgery don't die from suffocation.

Thank you.

***

LAWRENCE KAHN

CHENOWITH CASE

road construction bicycle crash rending woman a quadreplegic

LARRY KAHN
Seattle, WA

Larry Kahn has been representing individuals against insurance companies and institutions since 1986. He limits his practice to personal injury, wrongful death, medical malpractice, and elder negligence and abuse cases. Larry is an instructor at Keenan Ball College and has taught at all 3 locations: Atlanta, Austin, and Las Vegas.

At this point in his career, Kahn is able to focus his attention solely on helping seriously injured folks. When handling these cases — particularly when the loss of a loved one is involved — Kahn understands and appreciates the sensitive and sacred trust involved in seeking justice for the victims and their family. On each individual case, he and his entire staff work together tirelessly to seek the best results possible. They research, investigate, and hire the most authoritative and capable experts for every case they accept because their clients deserve the best.

Kahn was born in 1955, raised in Hillside, New Jersey, adjacent to Newark. In 1975, he moved to the Northwest to live, work and finish his undergraduate work, which had begun at Rutgers University. After completing his undergraduate degree, he attended law school and established a successful trial practice in the Los Angeles area for almost 15 years.

In 1999, he and his wife moved their family to the Seattle area to be closer to family and to once again enjoy the Great Northwest. Kahn established his Bellevue practice while still commuting to Los Angeles, thereby keeping his commitments to his former clients.

To date, Kahn's clients have prevailed in every jury trial, including several significant multi-million dollar verdicts and numerous significant defense verdicts. He has also successfully handled scores of arbitrations, mediations and settlements. In 1997, he was a featured attorney in "Verdicts and Settlements" for his $2.3 million verdict in *D.J. Chan's Investment Co. v. Robert and Elaine Chan*, Los Angeles Superior Court Case No. BC016734.

Kahn is licensed to practice law before all the state and federal courts in the states of Washington and California. He received his law degree from Southwestern University and his undergraduate degree from the University of Oregon School of Journalism.

(Opening Statement.)

PART I

Bicycle riding had the third highest Total Expenditures in Washington State by participants at $3.1 Billion Dollars, according to the 2015 'Economic Analysis of Outdoor Recreation' prepared by a blue ribbon panel for the State Recreation and Conservation Office.

[IF no push back:]

Over 173 crashes a day in the U.S. are caused by unsafe road design, including narrow roads/shoulders and missing traffic signs/signals, this is according to a study by the National Highway Traffic Safety Administration.

PART II

What brings us here today to this King County Courthouse are simple safety rules that protect us all whenever we're on public roadways.

These safety rules...like all safety rules...only protect us...if jurors choose to enforce them:

Safety Rule No. 1: A city must use qualified civil engineers before making any change to its roads to prevent serious injury or death to all of us.

Safety Rule No. 2: A city must design out any dangerous conditions on its roads. If they can't design it out, a city must protect or warn against these dangerous conditions on its road to prevent serious injury or death to all of us.

PART III

Let me tell you what happened here:

The City of Mercer Island (MI) has approximately 66 bumps, MI police called speed bump/rain catches, to divert water located all across the Island.

No written plans, calculations or designs were created by MI for any of these 66 speed bump/rain catches, so we do not know who or when most of these 65+ bumps were put in.

These 66+ speed bump/rain catches are put in roadways used by drivers, motorcyclists, bicyclists, roller skaters, pedestrians; children, young people, middle aged people and older folks of all different abilities.

None of the 66+ bumps are painted, or have a sign warning anyone using the road that these street bumps exist.

These 66+ street bump/rain catches are all different shapes, sizes and angles. Some go all the way across the street, some only part way; some follow the road, some angle into the roadway.

The City of Mercer Island says these speed bump/rain catches are put in to control and divert water flow from rain.

The City of Mercer Island has never done any written studies to confirm that any of the 66 bumps control or divert water as they are intended to do.

The City of Mercer Island has never tested or studied the ordinary safety of these 66 speed bump/rain catches for all users of the road.

No city engineer ever signed his or her name approving any one of these speed bump/rain catches.

Now let's focus on the speed bump/ rain catch located on Forest Avenue:

The City of Mercer Island hires Clint Morris, a <u>mechanical</u> engineering graduate, as an engineering intern in 1991. He works for the maintenance dept.

The City of Mercer Island gives Clint Morris the job title of "Street Engineer" in 2000, without Clint Morris ever earning a civil engineering degree, or receiving a professional engineering license.

Morris continues to work for the maintenance department.

Clint Morris is the supervisor for last minute, add-on work to be performed on the north side of Forest Avenue toward the end of this project in early 2004.

There are NO plans or specifications for this "add-on" work. Nothing is signed by a licensed, professional engineer.

Clint Morris decides to control rain run-off by adding a speed bump/rain catch in the road. He makes no calculations. He prepares no drawings or plans; he prepares no written design. He doesn't seek or receive any professional civil engineering approval.

Clint Morris eye-balled the street to determine the location and design of the bump based only on how he saw the water flow.

Clint Morris's work crew builds this bump by hand and eye, like all other bumps he has seen built, with the same color asphalt as the street.

Clint Morris knows as he did this that Forrest Avenue was a narrow street, and that cars drove up the middle of the street in both directions, having to move over or yield if cars were parked on portions of the street.

Clint Morris knows when he did this that he placed it at the bottom of the hill, where anything on wheels would be going fastest.

Clint Morris knows when he did this that he placed it at the bottom of the hill, where leaves and foliage collect and cover the speed bump/rain catch. Clint Morris knows when he did this that he placed it at the bottom of the hill where leaves would cover it and shadow and light from afternoon sun essentially would camouflage the bump.

Please take a look at the Police photograph taken of the scene. [blow up]

Now look at one taken a little closer. [blow up]

I see you might be having difficulty seeing it. It's right there up the road a bit from the mailboxes. Now picture a car coming up the middle of the road, and a bicyclist coming down the hill and moving over to the right. Where's the bump?

Now let me introduce you to our client, Margarete Chenoweth. She was a 48-year-old pre-school teacher who was paralyzed after unintentionally striking this speed bump/rain catch while riding her bicycle. Her husband David and their three children are clients as well.

The simple truth is, thoughtless construction makes troubles and destruction.

PART IV

Let me tell you who we are suing and why. We are suing The City of Mercer Island for <u>five</u> reasons.

Reason No. 1: Mercer Island violated the safety rule that requires all cities to use a licensed civil engineer before making any substantial change to its roads.

We know Mercer Island violated this safety rule because Mercer Island chose to use Clint Morris in the design and construction of this bump. Mercer Island chose to have him determine by himself that this bump was the most effective solution at diverting water at this location.

Clint Morris concedes he gave no thought of safety for all foreseeable users of the road. His job was to move water.

Why did MI used an unlicensed engineer to do this? Well, you don't have to wait for an answer. MI told us through its Head Engineer: What's it about? Saving money.

Mercer Island concedes it saves money to have a nonprofessional engineers do this design work. Mercer Island concedes that it has never done any engineering review of these 66+ this speed bump/rain catches, including the one we're here about today. Mercer Island concedes there are no written analyses, calculations, plans or drawings for any of these 66+

speed bump/rain catches, including the one we're here about today.

Given all that, we know Mercer Island violated this No. 1 safety rule.

Reason No. 2: The second reason we are suing Mercer Island is for violating the safety rule, which requires a city to design out any dangerous conditions on its roads. If they can't design it out, a city must protect or warn against these dangerous conditions on its road to prevent serious injury or death to all of us.

Mercer Island concedes there was no attempt made to protect against this speed bump/rain catch. Mercer Island concedes the speed bump/rain catch was made with the identical colored asphalt used to pave the road. [Police Photo from Far] Mercer Island concedes that there are trees that line the street, which at different times cast shadows and sunlight across the narrow street where the bump is located, making it nearly disappear. Mercer Island concedes there are no street lights on the narrow street.

Mercer Island's head engineer testified that Mercer Island chose not to paint the bump for two reasons: First, because it believed it would create confusion for drivers, cyclists and other users of the road; and second, that a yellow bump could cause a motorist to drive off the road. [PAUSE – scan jury]

Mercer Island's assistant engineer testified that Mercer Island chose not to put a sign warning of the bump because too many signs can cause people ignore those signs. [PAUSE/scan jury/DRINK WATER]

Reasons No. 3 and 4: The third and fourth reasons we are suing Mercer Island are based on the two un-contradicted major truths in this case:

No. 3, the bottom line is, if this hazard hadn't been there, Margarete would not have hit it, would not be in a wheelchair, and none of us would be here.

No. 4 is the second major truth involving the City's alleged <u>purpose</u> for this speed bump/rain catch. That alleged purpose was to direct water into a ditch. The second major truth is that, despite what Mercer Island alleges, <u>this</u> <u>bump</u> <u>did</u> **not** <u>direct water into the ditch when covered with leaves, as it is most of the year.</u> You will hear and see evidence that proves that.

Reason No. 5: Lastly, we brought this lawsuit because the City of Mercer Island chose not to do a risk/benefit analysis before constructing the speed bump/rain catch. Meaning, the potential risks were not weighed against any potential benefit of constructing this bump. Whether you're a parent, a teacher, a road engineer or anyone when there is a danger or risk, as there is from this bump, you must always weigh the full extent of the danger by whatever benefit it brings. Mercer Island chose not to do this.

That is why we will be asking you to do what Mercer Island never did: Determine whether the bump's risk outweighed the benefit.

So let's first talk about these dangers for a minute.

Once again, it's an absolute truth that this bump can put someone in a wheelchair. If it can cause someone to become quadriplegic, we know it can maim, cause brain damage, or even kill someone.

Mercer Island knew that one of these 66 bumps had caused another bicyclist to break his clavicle and fracture his neck. (**Can we use this?**)

Mercer Island knows this is a residential street; home to families, retirees and children who use these streets to drive, cycle, run, walk and roller blade up and down. Given this, we know this could have been mayhem for anyone. It just happened to be Margarete.

[Uphill Photo]

Everyone concedes these risks are heightened when a bump like this one is placed at the bottom of a steep hill, at an uphill angle where trees can cover the street with dark shadows and leaves.

After exploring these dangers, we then explored the potential benefits.

You will hear how runoff water was going into nearby properties and MI and Clint Morris knew this long before the "add-on" repaving and building this thing. They had neighbor complaints even before the improvement project was even budgeted. But the simple truth is, it doesn't work.

But putting that aside; if the City had conducted a risk/benefit analysis, it would have known that the serious risks posed by this speed bump/rain catch warranted – at a minimum painting the bump, or putting up signs warning drivers, pedestrians, motorcyclists and bicyclists alike of the upcoming hazard. No such risk/benefit analysis was ever done.

A licensed civil engineer should always make safety first.

For these reasons, we filed suit against the city of Mercer Island.

[Good long drink.]

PART V

Before coming to trial, there were still more questions we needed answered.

No. 1: Was Clint Morris, who only had a mechanical engineering degree, qualified to design and build this bump without a formal civil engineering degree, license or proper supervision, with only his 10 years of on the job experience?

Our Road Engineering Expert explained to us that mechanical engineers are not civil engineers. They do not have the proper qualifications, and no amount of on-the-job training is going to fix that. It would be like asking a pediatrician to perform open heart surgery. They both went to medical school, but studied distinctly different classes, and no amount of on the job training can replace that underlying education.

Our Road Engineering Expert went on to tell us that this bump does not exist in any civil engineering book, text, study, manual or drawing that he is aware of in over 50 years of experience. It is too unsafe. Based on the total failure to consider users of the road including bicyclists, our expert found he was unqualified to design and build this speed bump/ rain catch. No qualified engineer ever would build it.

Next, No. 2: We then wanted to know what made this bump unsafe. In addition to the Licensed Professional Road engineer, we hired a biomechanical engineer, a bicycle safety engineer, a collision reconstruction expert and a human factors engineer to review the bump and to a person, all told us that because this speed bump/rain catch is so similar to a speed bump, <u>even under the best conditions</u> it should not be used at all, especially not at the bottom of a slope where the speed of a vehicle or bicycle would be the fastest.

Question No. 3: We had to ask before coming to trial was, what obligation did Mercer Island have to warn all road users including bicyclists of this bump? We knew that, because this was a narrow residential street, the <u>majority (but not all) of the folks using this road</u> would be familiar with the road and the bump. So why should a city have to paint or put up signs about a bump most of the residents knew about, or should have known about?

Our Human Factors Engineer, whose sole job it is to study how humans interact with our environment, examined that question. She explained to us that all of us rely on signs and visual cues, like painted stripes, to make us aware of hazards, both known and unknown. Because of this, Mercer Island should have, at a minimum, either painted the bump or put up a sign warning every one of the hazard.

For our next question, Question No. 4: We also wanted to know why other municipalities like Bellevue, Lynwood, Edmunds and Gig Harbor were apparently using these hazardous speed bumps/rain catches, too, so we asked all our experts about that. Every one of them said that two wrongs don't make it right and that it does not mean all, or any, are safe. Also, it was pointed out that the evolutionary nature of designed safety in our world, like the evolution of protections at a railroad crossing, means that the danger may be widespread before it can be stopped based on safety and common sense…1,000 wrongs still do not make a right.

This brought us to the final question, Question No. 5: When we were truly analyzing the merits of the case, we had to take a good look at Margarete's conduct. What did she know and what could she have done?

How could Margarete not have seen this bump? She lived at her father-in-law's place with her family on Forest Avenue for years before this wreck, and knew that the bump existed on the street because she, in the past, drove her car over it when another car was coming from the opposite direction. But, she NEVER went over that bump on her bicycle before. She even had warned her children to stay off it on their bikes.

We learned that most of the time when there are no cars coming up the road, most folks on bicycles like Margarete will ride down the center of the road. On this occasion, April 15, 2013, there was a car coming up the road in the opposite direction. You will hear from our Bicycle Safety Expert and our Collision Reconstruction Expert who rode over the bump, about the difficulty they experienced going over the jarring bump even knowing it was coming.

So how is it possible that she herself did not see the bump in that moment, on that day?

We first looked at the police photographs of the bump immediately following of the crash. [SHOW PHOTOS] From these, we saw the bump juts out into the road, the lane of travel about four feet. There are no sidewalks or shoulders. We saw that the bump is the same asphalt color as the road, that shadows and sunlight covered the street, and that leaves covered most of the bump.

We spoke to some of the EMTs, firemen, and police officers who responded that day. It turns out that the police had to brush the leaves off the bump to spray paint around it for their measurements and photos.

We then asked our Human Factors Engineer the same pressing question: How is it possible Margarete did not see this bump?

We know that Margarete was riding her bicycle home from teaching. We know the weather was clear, and it had not rained recently. We know she was wearing her helmet, sunglasses and was following all traffic safety laws as she approached her street.

[Uphill photo showing bend]

We know as she came around the bend, safely riding down the hill tapping her brakes, a car was approaching up the middle of the road. We know Margarete moved to the right to yield to the car. We know her focus was on the car, as she waved with her left hand to thank the approaching car for also moving over. We know she hit the bump.

As she laid there motionless against the post, according to a first responder and MI fireman, Margarete said that she "hit a bump in the road, lost control of the bike and collided with the mailboxes." She told her son Noah, who was the very first person to find her laying there, the same thing. She said the same thing consistently under oath in deposition. She has never wavered from this account of the events. She will tell you the same thing here.

Our Human Factors Engineer explained to us that this exact situation is why qualified engineers know we need visual warnings, such as painted stripes or signs. She ex plained that when we are forced to focus on one thing, like an approaching vehicle, our brains can only focus on that one thing, unless there are other visual cues, such as bright paint or signs that draw our attention to other hazards. She explained how this is true even when we have prior knowledge of a hazard. It's human nature.

That is how we came to understand how, even though Margarete had gone past the bump many times before, she did not and could not see it on this occasion given the circumstances.

This is how we concluded it is necessary that hazards like this, when they can't be designed out or guarded against, must have visual warnings, such as painted stripes or signs, similar to what we see on speed bumps in our communities, to warn all users of the road against the danger.

Despite this, you will hear Margarete admit some responsibility.

Again, the dirt simple truth is, thoughtless construction makes troubles and destruction.

[Drink water]

PART VI

This brings us to the final reason we are here and the most important part of this case: The misery and troubles this wreck has caused Margarete and her family.

You will hear evidence through an expert economist that the present cash value of Dr. Kawai's Safe Life Care Plan for Margarete's lifetime is $14,825,811.00. Again, this is to make sure that she receives the best medical care and assistance to extend her statistical life span, rather than becoming the self-fulfilling prophecy of a plan that doesn't take care for her needs under every circumstance after the kids move on and whether something happens so she must live on her own.

The economist will also provide the present cash value of Margarete's Loss of Earnings, as she will not be able to work, in the sum of $350,326.00.

But, we don't need jurors for simply adding up these numbers. No, your most important job will be to determine the intangibles, the value of her deep loss of enjoyment of life, mental anguish, self-esteem and privacy, the misery and troubles this wreck has caused Margarete and her family. This will be, by far, your most important job.

She's a quadriplegic. While her family is thankful she is alive, you will hear Margarete describe her total and complete desperation, isolation and dependence on others. This once extremely independent, athletic, energetic woman who inspired all, who was the mom who got the kids away from the technology to go hiking, biking, skiing, etc., is totally dependent on everyone for everything. Every day is the same. Same routine. Same struggles.

MARK HENNESS

GILL CASE

Package truck pedestrian wrongful death

MARK HENNESS
Las Vegas, NV

Mark G. Henness was born and raised in Beaverton, Ore., birthplace of Nike and home to its world headquarters. He first came to Las Vegas to attend the University of Nevada, Las Vegas, where he graduated with distinction with a Bachelor's Degree in Theatre Arts. He returned to Oregon, where he attended law school at Willamette University College of Law, a private law school with the distinction of being the oldest law school west of the Mississippi. Henness earned his Juris Doctorate in 1995 and subsequently returned to Las Vegas to begin his law career. Mark is an instructor at Keenan Ball College and has taught at all 3 locations: Atlanta, Austin, and Las Vegas.

Henness' legal career began at the Nevada Attorney General's Office where he defended such entities as the Nevada Department of Transportation. Thereafter, Henness took a position with the regional law firm of Broening, Oberg Woods, Wilson & Cass, where his practice focused primarily on insurance defense and insurance bad faith defense.

Since 2000, Henness has been an owner and partner of Henness & Haight, Injury Attorneys. His practice has been dedicated solely to representing individuals injured in accidents. Henness has successfully tried numerous cases to verdict, and he handles all types of personal injury cases from motor vehicle injury cases to defective product cases. He has successfully collected millions of dollars from insurance companies on behalf of his clients.

In his spare time, Henness enjoys spending time with his wife and four children, playing tennis and golf, playing guitar, and performing close-up magic.

Part I

Every year nearly 3,000 people are killed and 400,000 more are injured due **to intentional, distracted driving** according to the National Highway Traffic Safety Administration.

What brings us to the Clark County Courthouse **today** are the **safety rules** that protect all of us from distracted driving. These safety rules…*like all safety rules*…only protect us if juries choose to enforce them.

Safety Rule #1: Companies must <u>make sure</u> their delivery drivers are qualified when hired and <u>remain qualified to drive</u> to protect all of us from serious injury and death.

Safety rule #2: Delivery drivers must see what is in front of them… and not drive intentionally distracted…to protect *all* of us from serious injury and death.

Safety Rule #3: Companies must put safety *before* their delivery quota system to protect all of us from serious injury and death.

Part II

Now let me tell you the story of what happened in this case.

Defendant UPS is the largest package delivery company in the world.

UPS has more than 100,000 package drivers on the road that deliver more than 18 million packages daily to businesses and homes.

Here in Las Vegas in 2003, UPS promotes one of its conveyor belt workers to delivery driver.

Before putting him on the road, driver is trained.

This training includes how to safely drive his truck when making deliveries to businesses and homes.

Some of the safe driver training comes from the UPS 340 E Methods.

CLICK

UPS trains its drivers to **look for pedestrians** as they return to the truck after a delivery.

CLICK to 340 Method Title Slide again that's blank

UPS also trains its drivers when it is and is **not** safe to look at their hand held computer, called a DIAD. The DIAD has a screen that tells the driver their next several delivery stops. The information on the screen is called EDD, or enhanced DIAD download.

CLICK MOVE OUT WITHOUT DELAY INSTRUCTIONS

UPS trains its driver not to look at their hand held computer, or DIAD, after getting back into the truck. UPS trains drivers to put away the DIAD as they are getting back into the driver's seat.

After being trained, UPS puts Driver on the road.

In order to make sure drivers meet delivery performance expectations, UPS uses a progressive discipline system.

CLICK;

The first step of the formal discipline process CLICK is a documented talk with. If the issue continues, the next step CLICK is a warning letter, followed by CLICK suspension and CLICK termination. UPS documents all formal discipline in a driver's qualification file.

CLICK TO BLANK

GO TO BINDER

PICK UP DRIVER FILE AND PUT IT ON TABLE

This is the driver qualification file we received from UPS and the evidence will show that it proves what happened in the case.

HOLD BINDER

Nov 1, 2004: Driver hits something *he doesn't see* while backing. (1)

Tap binder

20 months later (July 24, 2006), driver *again*…hits something he doesn't see while backing. (2)

Tap binder.

Less than a year later, (April 6, 2007) UPS observes driver not following his training **when pulling away from a delivery stop**. (3)

Tap binder

Three weeks later, (April 25, 2007) UPS again observes driver not following his training when pulling away from a stop. (5)

Tap Binder

17 months later (September 11, 2008), driver's truck is hit. UPS says driver **did not**

properly check the area around his truck when he parked. (6)

Tap binder

That same month (September 15, 2008), driver's supervisor goes with driver on his route. During the ride, supervisor has to remind driver to **completely stop at all stop signs and to stop behind cross walks.** Supervisor also must remind Driver to *look for pedestrians when returning to his truck*. (7)

Tap binder

Two months later (November 10, 2008) during another ride, supervisor again has to **remind driver to look for pedestrians when returning to his truck** and to *"stay more alert."* (8)

Tap binder

A week later…November 17, 2008… supervisor again has to remind driver to look for pedestrians when returning to his truck and to "stay alert." (9)

Tap binder

Two weeks later (December 1, 2008) supervisor again observes and documents driver not properly stopping at stop signs and cross walks.

Move to Corporate Structure

Show Corp Structure

Back to Binder

Tap binder

In February 2009, (February 18-20, 2009) supervisor Josh Church goes with driver on a 3 day supervised **safety** ride. Supervisor Church observes and ***212*** infractions committed by Driver of his UPS training, including numerous infractions for looking at his DIAD inside his truck. (10.5)

11. Tap binder

Two weeks later in March 2009 (March 3, 2009) supervisor Church again observes Driver **not looking for pedestrians when returning to his truck**.

MOVE TO POWER POWER POINT

PERFORMANCE DISCIPLINE TIMELINE

CLICK

CLICK UP

Next, April 29, 2009, UPS brings driver into the office for a **documented "talk-with"**, part of the UPS progressive discipline process, BECAUSE **he is taking too long** to finish his route. UPS tells Driver he needs to finish the week strong so he doesn't "put himself in the position to be back in the office in regards to his performance."

CLICK DOWN

CLICK UP

Two weeks later, (May 15, 2009) UPS again brings driver into the office for another documented "talk-with."

CLICK DOWN

CLICK UP

Three weeks later (June 4, 2009), UPS again brings driver into the office, documents more discipline and tells driver his performance is unacceptable, *because he is not working fast enough.*

CLICK DOWN

CLICK UP

One month later (July 1, 2009), UPS issues driver a formal warning letter, the next step in the progressive discipline process. The warning letter documents driver's continued unacceptable performance *for not working fast enough* and cites six previous times that he had been talked with about his unacceptable performance. Driver is warned that continued unacceptable performance will result in further discipline, including termination.

CLICK DOWN

BACK TO BINDER

NO CLICK

Less than three months later month later, September 2009, (September 1-3, 2009) Supervisor Church goes with driver on another 3 day supervised **safety** ride. Supervisor observes *165* infractions by Driver of his UPS training, including numerous infractions for looking at his DIAD inside his truck.

BACK TO POWER POINT

CLICK UP

Less than two weeks later, (September 14, 2009) UPS again brings driver into the office and documents more discipline. Driver is told he needs to improve, meaning work faster, or they will be having "a different conversation."

CLICK DOWN

NO CLICK

According to Supervisor Church, sometime in 2009, UPS starts using a delivery quota, which UPS calls SPORH, "stops per on road hour." Using the SPORH, or quota, UPS expects drivers to *average* **a minimum number of delivery stops each hour during**

their shift. The quota is set for each driver during supervised rides based on the driver's "best-demonstrated performance." Once the quota is set, UPS expects drivers to maintain that average number of stops while working unsupervised. UPS says drivers can meet their SPOHR, or quota, by following their driver training. If the quota is not met, it is because the driver is not following his training. UPS tells its drivers that not meeting their SPORH, or quota, will result in discipline.

NO CLICK

Driver's SPORH or quota is set at 18 stops per hour each hour of his shift.

CLICK UP

Shortly after, (October 30, 2009), UPS issues driver a **second formal warning letter**, this time for not meeting his delivery quota. The letter warns driver that continued unacceptable performance ***for not making enough stops each hour*** will result in further discipline, including termination.

CLICK DOWN

NO CLICK

A few days later (November 3, 2009), UPS sends Supervisor Church back out on the road with driver.

PICK UP EMAIL FOR JURY

Church document the following in Driver's file after the ride:

Read Parts of Email

BACK TO POWER POINT

CLICK UP

Five months later (March 30, 2010), driver doesn't meet his quota. UPS disciplines driver.

CLICK DOWN

CLICK UP

Two months later (May 20, 2010), driver doesn't meet his quota. UPS disciplines driver.

CLICK DOWN

NO CLICK

BACK TO BINDER

TAP BINDER

A week later (May 26, 2010) UPS observes driver not looking around his vehicle for pedestrians.

TAP BINDER

A few days later (June 1, 2010), UPS business manager Morgan Tolliver goes on a 1-day ride with Driver, and OBSERVES 109 more infractions by driver of his training including numerous violations for looking at his DIAD, or quota machine, after getting back into his truck.

BACK TO POWER POINT

CLICK UP

Two days later, Driver gets a **third formal warning letter** for not working fast enough or meeting his delivery quota. He is told if this continues, it would result in further discipline, including discharge.

CLICK DOWN

BACK TO BINDER

NO CLICK

Two months later, in August 2010 (August 11-12, 16), Supervisor Church goes back out again on the road with driver. Over three consecutive work-days, Josh Church observes over **380** infractions by driver of his UPS training. These infractions include repeated violations for not looking for pedestrians when returning to his truck and repeated violations for looking at his DIAD, **_or quota machine_**, after getting back into his truck. Church also notes Driver "looks confused at times." Church tells Driver he needs to keep pushing forward.

BACK TO POWER POINT

CLICK UP

Following this three-day ride (August 17, 2010), UPS increases driver's delivery quota from 18 to 23 stops per hour, or roughly 40 more stops **PER DAY**. Let me repeat that. UPS increases driver's quota by roughly 40 more stops **PER DAY**.

CLICK DOWN

CLICK UP

Two weeks later (August 31, 2010), UPS again disciplines driver for not meeting his quota. UPS issues Driver a **fourth warning letter** (September 2, 2010) and again tells Driver if he doesn't work faster, he will receive further discipline, including discharge.

CLICK DOWN

CLICK UP

A week later (September 8, 2010), UPS again disciplines driver for not meeting his quota.

CLICK DOWN

CLICK UP

A week later (September 14, 2010-referrenced in 9/22 letter), UPS **suspends** Driver for one day for not meeting his delivery quota the previous week.

CLICK DOWN

CLICK UP

The following week (September 22, 2010), UPS again disciplines driver for not meeting his quota and tells him he needs to increase his performance over the next three days to meet his quota.

CLICK DOWN

CLICK UP

Less than two months later (November 4, 2010), UPS again disciplines driver for not meeting his quota.

CLICK DOWN

CLICK UP

Five days later (November 9, 2010), UPS again disciplines driver for not meeting his quota.

CLICK DOWN

BACK TO BINDER

TAP BINDER

A few months later (January 4, 2011), UPS again observes driver not looking for pedestrians when he returns to his truck.

BACK TO POWER POINT

CLICK to CHANGE TIMELINE TO PART 2

CLICK UP

Two months later (February 23, 2011), UPS disciplines driver for not meeting his quota.

CLICK DOWN

NO CLICK

Show Corp structure again to introduce KG

BACK TO BINDER

Tap binder

In May 2011 (May 3-5 2011), driver's next supervisor, Karl Groneman, goes out with driver on another three-day supervised ride. During this three-day period, Supervisor Groneman observes 305 more infractions by driver of his UPS training. These include violations for looking at his DIAD, *__or quota machine__*, after returning to his truck.

BACK TO POWER POINT

CLICK UP

Following the ride, UPS keeps driver's quota locked in at 23 stops per hour.

CLICK DOWN

CLICK UP

Two months later (July 5, 2011), UPS again disciplines driver for not meeting his quota. UPS tells Driver he was off by more than a stop per hour.

CLICK DOWN

CLICK UP

One week later (July 12, 2011), UPS again disciplines driver for not meeting his quota.

CLICK DOWN

CLICK UP

Two weeks later (July 26, 2011), same thing.

CLICK DOWN

BACK TO BINDER

Tap Binder

One week later (August 1, 2011), Supervisor Groneman goes back out with driver on a one-day supervised ride and observes 48 more infractions by driver of his training. Supervisor Groneman tells Driver "work smarter, not harder." Supervisor Groneman also documents Driver's frustration with his route and Driver tells Supervisor Groneman he knows his route impacts his SPORH.

STORY OF WHAT HAPPENED

Three months later

Wednesday

November 8, 2011.

Clear, sunny day. Approximately 3:15 in the afternoon.

Residential neighborhood. Henderson.

Driver drives his delivery truck into this neighborhood,

CLICK

a neighborhood that is on his normal route, and which he has driven in many times before.

It is a neighborhood with families and children.

It is a neighborhood where half the residents have to cross the street to get their mail, which the UPS driver knew.

Driver stops on the right side of the street at 2502 Swan Ridge Avenue, a residential street with houses on both sides.

He grabs a package and exits his truck with the package and his hand held computer.

Driver delivers the package at the front door of 2502.

Driver goes back to his truck, gets in and sits down.

Driver looks at his hand held computer.

Driver pulls away from the curb and accelerates.

He drives 110 feet, reaching a speed of approximately 21 MPH.

The front middle of his truck hits something in the middle of the street.

He then slams on the brakes and skids 18 feet to a stop.

The impact he feels is the front, middle of his UPS truck striking a person who is in the middle of the street.

The person is knocked **34** feet down the street.

The driver gets out of his truck, sits down on the curb, and calls UPS.

A neighbor calls 911.

A motorcycle officer and ambulance arrive first.

The person is transported to the hospital and pronounced dead.

CLICK

The person is 69 year-old Margery Gill,

CLICK

A person who lived in that neighborhood who was crossing the street to her mailbox that was directly across from her driveway.

We represent Ms. Gill's estate and her brothers. We are their lawyers.

If you remember one thing, remember this: A UPS driver like this ONLY remains behind the wheel *because of a system failure.*

Part III

We are suing UPS for 2 reasons and the UPS driver, for 1:

First, we are suing UPS for *violating* the safety rule that requires companies to make sure its drivers are qualified when hired and remain qualified to drive. We know UPS violated this rule for several reasons. We know UPS knew driver had a history of not looking for pedestrians. We know UPS knew driver had a history of looking at his DIAD, his quota machine, after getting back

into his truck. We also know UPS observed over 1100 violations over 13 supervised days in just the three years before he struck and killed Ms. Gill.

Ladies and gentlemen, it wasn't a matter of if…it was ONLY a matter of WHEN.

We also know the quota, or SPORH, was an expectation of the job. UPS says drivers can hit their quota if they follow their training.

If you believe that's true, then for every instance of formal discipline, all of the documented "talk-withs" warning letters and suspension, UPS knew driver was not following his training. Therefore, the evidence shows he was not qualified to drive.

In addition to seeing all of these documents, you will hear from Joshua Church and what he observed.

CLICK

Play Church clip fumbling with his DIAD

PAUSE 3 SECONDS

You will also hear Supervisor Church explain driver would get back into the truck and look at his DIAD, or quota machine. Supervisor Church will tell you this in an in-cab distraction and not safe.

CLICK;

Play Church clip looking at DIAD and not moving out

PAUSE 3 SECONDS

You will also hear from the driver, who will tell you he didn't know he wasn't supposed to look at his hand-held computer, his DIAD, after getting back into his truck from a delivery.

Play McCallum clip – I didn't know I wasn't supposed to use the DIAD.

PAUSE 3 SECONDS

CLICK

You will also hear that he didn't know he had a quota or SPORH requirement.

Play McCallum SPORH clip here

PAUSE 3 SECONDS

Given all of this, that is how we concluded UPS violated safety rule number one and knew driver was not qualified to be on the road when he struck and killed Ms. Gill.

Again, this wasn't a matter of if, but ONLY A MATTER OF WHEN.

We're also suing Driver McCallum because he violated safety rule #2 that requires all drivers to look ahead of them and not drive intentionally distracted.

We know Driver McCallum violated this safety rule because he did not see Ms. Gill until it was too late. We know this for several reasons: First, we know there are no skid marks before impact. *Let me repeat that, there are no skid marks before impact.* Second, we know, and you will hear, there was nothing obstructing Driver McCallum's view of Ms.

Gill as he accelerated toward her. Third, we know Ms. Gill was in the middle of the street when she was struck by the middle of his truck. We know this because you can see the make up from her face on the front of the truck.

And last, you will hear two different stories from Driver McCallum. In the first, you will hear how he told the first officer to arrive that he never saw Ms. Gill until after he hit her. In his second story, after UPS management arrived and met with driver, he told a second police officer he saw Ms. Gill right before he struck and killed her.

He also told the second officer that he was doing the UPS triangle method of checking his passenger side mirror, his left mirror and gauges when he struck and killed Ms. Gill.

Whichever story you choose to believe, that he didn't see her until after he hit her or he saw her right before he hit her, the simple truth is: had he been looking at the road, he would have seen her. That is how we know he violated the second safety rule and drove distracted.

The other reason we are suing UPS is because UPS violated the safety rule that requires companies to put safety before their delivery quota system.
Show Visual of Discipline
CLICK
LADIES AND GENTLMEN, LET ME BE CLEAR, WE WILL SHOW YOU EACH AND EVERY ONE OF THESE DOCUMENTS. THEY WILL BE INTRODUCED AND SHOWN TO YOU DURING THIS TRIAL and they will be given to you to help guide you in your deliberations.
The bottom line is: UPS only disciplined this driver when he did not meet his quota and never disciplined the driver for violating his safety training, including not looking for pedestrians and looking at his DIAD *or quota machine* when he got back in his truck.

That is how we were able to conclude UPS violated safety rule number 3 and put their quota system before safety.

CLICK TO BLANK SLIDE BEFORE TTD

Part IV

Now before coming here, there were several other things we had to figure out in order to decide whether to bring it before a jury like you.

When looking at this case, we needed to know what Ms. Gill was doing that day. In order to know that, we needed to learn about who she was. What we learned was she was a 5'7" 69 year old woman. We learned she had no mobility issues; she was an avid walker who was often seen in her neighborhood picking up trash to help keep it clean. We learned she was a retired second grade teacher who spent 30 years in the Clark County School District and had continued to tutor children until she was killed.

We spoke with Ms. Gill's friends and Pastor. We found out she was a devout Catholic, and that on very day she was killed she was on her way to meet her Pastor to organize some help for the community. We also learned she had just recently purchased a plane ticket to be with her family for Christmas.

We also learned she wore glasses and that she was wearing them when she killed. We learned she was not on her phone or wearing headphones when she went to cross her street. According to the police, the only thing found at the scene was her keys. There was no mail.

We spoke to the investigating officer. He told us that Ms. Gill walked out of her open garage, down her driveway and was walking to her mailbox when she was hit. He also told us Ms. Gill had no alcohol or drugs in her system when she was killed.

He also told us Ms. Gill was hit by the front of the UPS truck. He knows this because the makeup she was wearing was found of the front of the UPS truck.

The officer also told us the UPS truck accelerated to 21 miles per hour in just over 100 feet when it struck Ms. Gill.

The officer also told us Ms. Gill was in the line of sight of the UPS driver the entire time he accelerated toward her.

*We also hired D.I. to look at the case. **HE IS A RECONSTRUCTIONIST**. He told us that an average driver with average reaction time could have seen and avoided hitting Ms. Gill if HE WAS just looking where HE WAS going.*

From all of this evidence it will be for you decide whether when Ms. Gill walked down her drive way, she saw the parked UPS truck and believed it would be safe for her to cross.

PART V-VII

This then brings us to the final reason you're here and that is learning who Margery Gill was and what impact her death has had on her family. Our job is to provide you with the tools to help you figure those things out and that's why we will bring forth people who will tell you who she was. This includes neighbors, co-workers, church members and her family members.

Now as to damages in the case, ladies and gentlemen, Nevada law is very clear, and let me now point out the specific damages in this case. First, compensatory means to compensate the survivors for the loss of life. To that end, you will have the testimony from some folks who knew Ms. Gill's, her background and passions, and what she meant to the survivors. Next, you will understand that the law recognizes pain and suffering prior to death. And to assist you in determining how much time there was, **let me show you this time line.** CLICK

This time line will be used during the trial to help you understand what the witnesses saw prior to death.

CLICK DOWN TIME LINE

The second purpose of Nevada's compensation laws is to deter the wrongdoer. LET ME BE VERY CLEAR. That does NOT mean additional money. It means a full, complete and fair compensatory verdict must be given in order to deter the wrongdoer from doing this again. If you cut it down or in any way discount the verdict, it will not deter the things that have happened here from happening again.

The final area of damages, which does not occur in all cases, but does occur when the corporate or other defendant's conduct is ***so reckless*** as to constitute ***a conscious disregard for the safety of others,*** and that is called punitive damages. On this issue you will be asked during, does the evidence warrant punitive damages and you will consider all the evidence in this case to make that decision.

So as you hear the evidence flow from the witness stand, keep in your mind's eye what evidence is there to prove this was preventable? As you do, consider this: Driver McCallum still drives for UPS today (and he still drivers today the way he drove on the day he struck and killed Ms. Gill.)

And one final matter which you may determine to be important on a multitude of issues, and that is the family that will receive the verdict--the compensatory, the pain and suffering, the punitive damages--will place every penny in a non-profit foundation for the advancement of teachers and elementary education. Every penny

Which brings us to the last, but very important matter I need to visit with you about. And that is, ladies and gentlemen, at some point, maybe right now, maybe early next week, or at the end the case, the question will strike you: why…why did this happen? It is a reasonable question and one you should be asking. And this is particularly important here because you are being asked to consider whether punitive damages are necessary. So when asking yourself why this happened, or *what was root cause for why this happened,* you may want to consider two things. There are more, but consider these: Number one: why did UPS choose only to discipline for quota violations and not safety violations? And two: Why did UPS choose to keep this driver on the road?

And as you are considering these things and as you listen to the evidence, somewhere along the way you may be asking yourself, this sounds like profits over people. But respectfully that is for you to decide.

OPENING TEMPLATE

OPENING TEMPLATE

- STATISTIC

- PURPOSE

- SAFETY RULES

- STORY

- WHO WE ARE SUING AND WHY

- DISARMING DEFENSES

- DAMAGES AND LOSSES